THE WAYFARER'S JOURNEY

A Doctor's Memoir of
Exile, Psychiatry, and Meaning

Vincent Abad, M.D.

ADVANCED MEMORY AND PSYCH SOLUTIONS
PUBLISHER

Praise for The Wayfarer's Journey

"It is with deep admiration and heartfelt gratitude that I endorse *The Wayfarer's Journey* to all who walk alongside the most vulnerable among us, and to one extraordinary man who has led that journey with unwavering compassion: Dr. Vincent Abad.

When I first met Dr. Abad, Caridad Center had no formal mental health program. We recognized the need but lacked the structure, resources, and leadership to bring it to life. Through his tireless vision, dedication, and fierce commitment to serving the underserved, Dr. Abad built a mental health program that now serves thousands in our community, restoring dignity, hope, and healing to those who had long been forgotten.

This memoir highlights Dr. Abad's courage and dedication, from his war-torn childhood to his career focused on compassion. His story is not only a testament to resilience but also a call to action for all of us in the fields of care, justice, and service.

Knowing Dr. Abad has been one of the greatest honors of my life. **His legacy lives on through the lives he has touched with his wisdom, kindness, and generous spirit."**

—Connie Berry, Founder, Caridad Center, Boynton Beach, Florida

"I've had the privilege of knowing Dr. Vincent Abad for over a decade, both as a compassionate physician and a thoughtful human being. He treated my mother during her struggle with dementia, and through that deeply personal connection, I came to admire not only his clinical skill but also his profound humanity.

Over the years, our conversations have often turned to philosophy, history, and the deeper questions of life. In *The Wayfarer's Journey*, Dr. Abad brings that same depth and insight to the page. **His memoir reflects an extraordinary life of exile, service, and moral clarity. It explores what it means to be truly human in a world often influenced by greed and selfishness.**

Dr. Abad writes with the quiet force of someone who has lived, listened, and learned. This book will resonate with anyone who has wrestled with exile, injustice, and the enduring hope of freedom and meaning. It is a rare gift—a memoir that both challenges and uplifts, that reveals as much about the reader as it does about the author. I recommend it without reservation."

—Ray Leon, Co-CEO of Outpace Systems, Inc.

"It has been my great privilege to know Dr. Vincent Abad for many years, through both professional collaboration and personal friendship. We've cared for mutual patients and exchanged ideas across disciplines, and throughout that time, I've come to admire not only his clinical skill but also the depth of his humanity. Dr. Abad is a physician of uncommon dedication, with a clear moral compass and a profound respect for the people he serves.

Beyond medicine, our friendship has grown through countless conversations about history, immigration, politics, and the many forces that shape the human experience. These exchanges have always left me with a sense of gratitude and reflection. Dr. Abad is a thoughtful and engaged citizen of the world, someone who brings wisdom, empathy, and insight to every interaction.

In *The Wayfarer's Journey,* he brings those same qualities to the page. **This memoir provides an honest look at a life shaped by movement across countries, roles, and ideas, highlighting the meaning discovered throughout the journey. It is a story that will resonate with anyone who has wrestled with identity, purpose, and the cost of exile. I am honored to support this work and the man behind it."**

—Dr. Leon Poveda, Community Health Center, Florida Atlantic University

"As a compassionate healthcare provider, I found *The Wayfarer's Journey* to be a profoundly moving and necessary read. This memoir is more than a story of exile and healing—it's a testament to the resilience of the human spirit and the transformative power of compassionate care. Through the lens of personal struggle and professional dedication, the author invites us into a journey that is both intimate and universal.

What makes this book so inspiring is its honest reflection on what it means to serve others while navigating one's own pain. It challenges us—as caregivers, leaders, and fellow humans—to listen more deeply, to lead with empathy, and to never lose sight of the meaning behind our work. The narrative is beautifully written, rich with insight, and grounded in a deep understanding of the emotional and ethical complexities of healthcare.

This memoir is a call to action for all of us in the healing professions: to be better listeners, more present providers, and more courageous advocates for those we serve. It reminded me why I chose this path and renewed my commitment to walk it with compassion and purpose."

—Cameron Duncan, Ph.D., DNP, APRN, FNP-C, PMHNP-BC, CNE, FAANP
Eminent Dean of the School of Nursing, Florida Atlantic University

This is a work of nonfiction. The events and reflections presented here are based on the author's memory, experience, and interpretation. Some names and identifying details have been changed to respect the privacy of individuals. Any medical or psychological commentary reflects the author's professional insights but is not intended as clinical advice.

Cover Image: *The Wayfarer* by Hieronymus Bosch, circa 1500.
This painting, also known as *The Pedlar*, is widely seen as a reflection on humankind's moral journey. **The central figure represents Man navigating life's journey while resisting temptations, symbolized by the brothel in the background.** Themes of exile, wandering, and moral reflection make *The Wayfarer* a meaningful visual companion to this memoir. Image sourced from *Wikimedia Commons*. This image is in the public domain and can be freely reproduced without restriction.

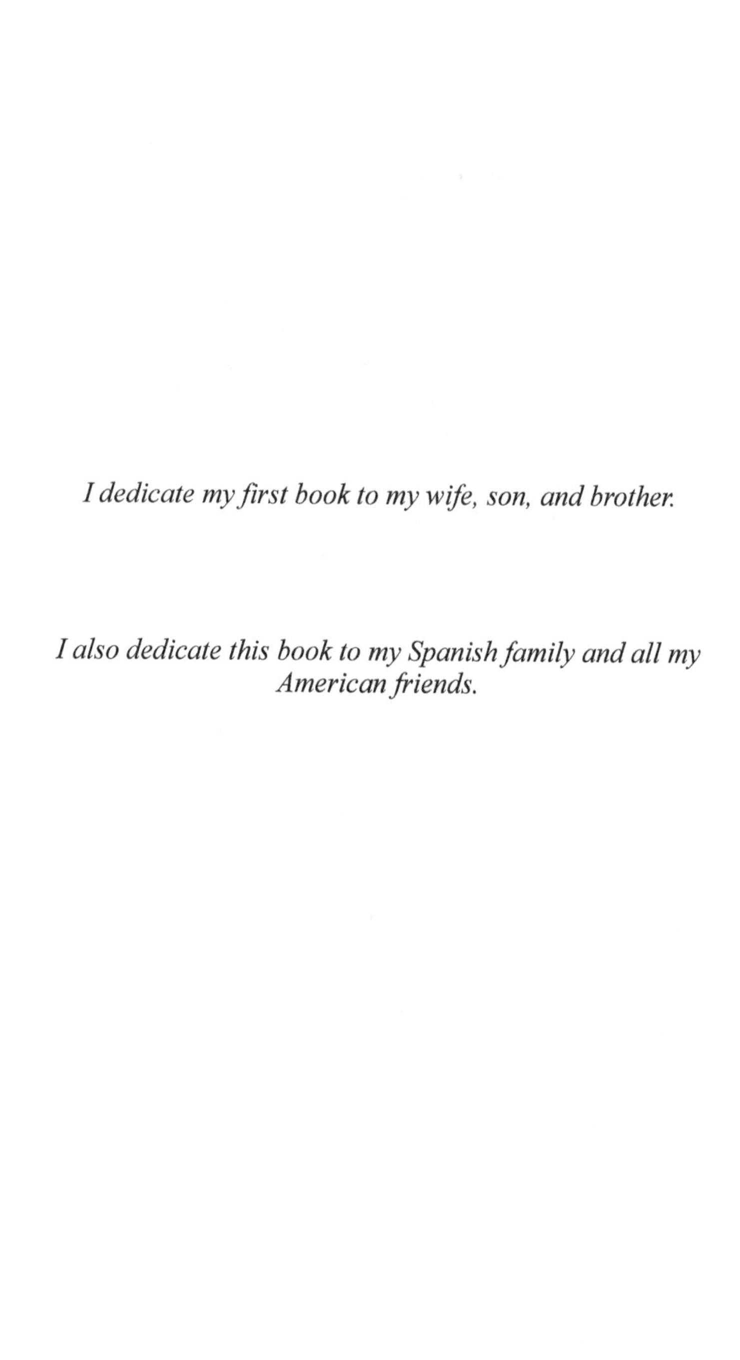

I dedicate my first book to my wife, son, and brother.

I also dedicate this book to my Spanish family and all my American friends.

*"Go confidently in the
direction of your dreams.
Live the life you have imagined."*

—Henry David Thoreau

*"The meaning of life is to find your gift.
The purpose of life is to give it away."*

—Pablo Picasso

Contents

Prologue: Racing the Clock

Dear reader,

I don't know if I'll still be alive when you read this page. That's not a metaphor — it's a fact. I've already stared at the ceiling of an operating room, waiting for a surgeon's hand to decide whether my story would continue or end. One slip, one moment of inattention, and everything I've lived, loved, or learned could have vanished.

I survived that procedure. But survival is not the same as completion. Now I'm racing against a different kind of clock — the invisible one that ticks inside the restless mind of someone with ADHD. Focus eludes me, distractions multiply, and the finish line of this book seems to move each time I reach for it. Yet the urgency grows sharper day by day.

This memoir is not a quiet reflection written from the safety of distance. It is a confession written near the end of the race, with the will to live still in my lungs. It is my rebellion against hesitation and silence. While the music is still in me, I have come to see that my life holds stories and lessons that may be useful to others who are just beginning their journey, or who find themselves halfway through it.

For years, I did not write because I lacked confidence. I doubted what I had to say mattered. I was wrong. I decided to write this memoir first — to put it down honestly and without delay — before turning to another book that will distill my reflections, along with those of others, on medicine, psychiatry, and philosophy.

At its core, this book argues for the necessity of a moral compass. A life — and a society — cannot endure without one. A compass that places the welfare of all at its center: human beings, other living creatures, and the fragile environment that sustains us. Without that compass, personal lives fracture, institutions decay, and governments lose their way. With it, both private lives and public policies gain coherence, purpose, and resilience.

I share the conviction that there is still much in this world worth defending: beauty, compassion, and the efforts of countless people working to repair harm and reduce suffering. The task before us is not domination, but harmony — learning how to live responsibly within the living world that makes our existence possible.

Not long ago, I had another reminder of how fragile it all is. A car ran a red light and missed me by inches. One second earlier and this would be a posthumous work. That near collision didn't just frighten me; it awakened me. I realized how much I still want to share before I'm gone. Perhaps we are all living on borrowed time, but only a few of us stop pretending otherwise.

When we finally grasp that "later" may never come, something essential shifts. We begin to speak instead of waiting. We show up instead of planning. We write because silence has become unbearable.

So here I am, writing as a man who has lived through dictatorship and exile, who has practiced medicine and wrestled with its moral contradictions, who has searched for love, meaning, and redemption in a fractured world. This book is my offering — part memoir, part medicine, part act of resistance.

I have no illusions of perfection. What you hold is not a polished artifact but a living record of wonder and struggle — a conversation between the man I was and the man I am still becoming.

I don't have all the answers. But I have stories — of war and compassion, of loss and courage, of the quiet victories that make a life worth remembering. If even one of them touches you, then this race has meaning.

Introduction

I began writing this book to leave a trace — something lasting, a memory of my existence — for my family, my friends, and anyone who might one day open these pages in search of meaning. I wanted those who have known me to see beyond the professional titles, the laughter, and the silences, into the deeper currents that shaped my life. And for those just beginning their own pilgrimage or pausing, as I have, to ask what it all means and how we might still make a difference.

I've learned that the surest way to happiness is not through comfort or recognition but through service: giving one's time, mind, and heart to the wellbeing of others. It is there, in acts of compassion, that I have found healing and purpose — and it is that current of service that flows through every chapter of this memoir.

The image that guided me from the start was Hieronymus Bosch's *The Wayfarer* (circa 1500), now housed in the Museum Boijmans Van Beuningen in Rotterdam. I still remember the first time I stood before it. A lone traveler, worn and ragged, strides along a dusty road with his patched cloak flapping like a flag of endurance. One hand grips a staff, both weapon and crutch, while the other steadies a basket heavy with invisible burdens: memory, guilt, responsibility, and perhaps hope. Behind him, chaos brews: a crumbling tavern spills laughter, lust, and drunken song; a man urinates against the wall while a couple embraces in the window. Above it all, an owl peers down, not as a sage but as a mocking sentinel of folly. A snarling dog nips at the traveler's heels as if daring him to turn back.

Bosch, that mischievous moralist, turned life into allegory. Every inch of his canvas teems with symbols — the magpie of impiety, pigs of overindulgence, a birdcage of spiritual confinement. But what arrests me most is not the grotesquerie. It's the man himself — the solitary traveler moving forward through a perilous landscape, refusing to surrender to despair or distraction. He is not just Bosch's creation. He is all of us.

In the fifteenth century, sin was measured by theology. Today, our demons wear subtler disguises. The brothel behind the traveler could just as well be the seductive glow of consumerism, the endless scroll of digital noise promising connection but breeding emptiness. The snapping dog becomes the restless anxiety of modern life. The owl, once a false prophet, may now stand for misinformation, moral apathy, or the corrosion of truth. The landscape has changed, but the journey remains the same: how to move forward through temptation, fear, and confusion without losing one's soul.

That is the enduring power of Bosch's vision and the pulse of this memoir. My own life has been a long and winding pilgrimage: from the silent streets of Franco's Spain to the fluorescent corridors of American hospitals, from exile and loss to discovery and service. Along the way I have carried my share of burdens and doubts but also luminous moments and encounters that revealed something indestructible about the human spirit's capacity for renewal.

Bosch's wayfarer reminds me that life is not a random wandering but a moral path — one that demands vigilance, humility, and compassion. We may never escape the burdens we carry, but we can decide how to bear them and for whom. We can choose again and again between fear and freedom, cynicism and hope, illusion and truth.

This book is my humble tribute to that choice. It is an offering to the road itself, and to the travelers who walk beside me. I have tried to capture not only the milestones of a life in medicine and exile, but the enduring questions that arise: What does it mean to serve? To love? To remain awake in a sleeping world?

If these pages help you pause and breathe, if they stir in you a renewed courage to keep walking your own road with tenderness and conviction, then my purpose will have been fulfilled.

And so, dear reader, take my hand. The way ahead is long, but the light flickers on the horizon.

Let us walk together.

Part I.
SPAIN

"Spain is a country that is always searching for itself."

—Juan Goytisolo

Chapter 1:
Born under Fire

*"War does not determine who is right—
only who is left."*
—Bertrand Russell

The Place and Year I Was Born

I was born in the middle of a civil war.

On June 22, 1937, while Spain was tearing itself apart, I came into the world in a small whitewashed village called Gestalgar, in the hills west of Valencia. There were no lullabies. There was no peace. What reached my cradle was the low, distant sound of artillery. Not close enough to kill us, but close enough to remind everyone that death was nearby. My pregnant mother, stubborn and determined, had escaped to the remote, stony hills of Valencia, where the air smelled of pine, rosemary, and wood smoke, rather than gunpowder.

My brother Pepe was less fortunate. He stayed behind in Mislata with our Aunt Josephine, not far from Valencia. He still shudders when he recalls those nights. The sirens wailed like a desperate chorus warning of death overhead. Families scrambled in the darkness, clutching children and rosaries, rushing to shelters as fear thickened the air.

"The whole house trembled," Pepe once told me, his voice still edged with that terror. "We thought the roof would collapse on us. You could hear the bombs falling closer. Boom, boom, boom."

Above them, German and Italian planes unspooled their deadly cargo, shaking the earth until walls cracked and nerves frayed. Valencia was then the temporary center of the Republic's government, and so it became the bullseye of fascism's fury.

My father was far from home, fighting with the Republican Army on the Teruel front, defending the fragile but noble idea that Spain could be a democracy. My mother defended something quieter but just as urgent: the flame of a new life, hidden in the hills, in a country that seemed determined to kill its own people.

*

In the summer of 1936, Spain erupted. Cities burst with fury and ideals. In Madrid's cafés men argued late into the night about freedom and betrayal. Churches were sacked and burned; priests were shot. Politicians and intellectuals were hunted on both sides. The country cracked along invisible fault lines of class, faith, region, and memory.

The war started with a military uprising led by nationalist generals Francisco Franco, Emilio Mola, and José Sanjurjo on July 17, 1936 against the democratically elected Second Republic. Franco became the leader of the insurgent forces which only partly succeeded. Some joined the insurgents while others refused. What followed was not a swift coup but a drawn-out civil war that devoured its own people — the most destructive conflict Europe had seen since World War I.

The war was ignited by political polarization between left-wing and right-wing factions, deep economic hardship, a string of political assassinations, and the victory of the left-wing Popular Front in the February 1936 elections.

Madrid came under siege, and the government retreated to Valencia, becoming the site of the last refuge of a desperate government, a coalition led by Manuel Azaña. Francisco Largo Caballero was the first prime minister, followed by Juan Negrín. The government, characterized by hope and contradictions, was an uneasy alliance of republicans, anarchists, socialists, communists, and nationalists from Catalonia and the Basque Country — all who were desperately trying to save a progressive vision of Spain that was now crumbling.

Even in those dark days, Spain offered the world a glimmer of hope by appointing its first cabinet minister,

Federica Montseny, an anarchist and intellectual, as Minister of Health and Social Assistance, who embodied the progressive dream. She was not only the first woman in Europe to hold such a post but she spoke of hospitals, birth control, and social reform while bombs were falling on her city.

But the Republic's dream was cracking from within. Deep ideological fractures splintered the unity. In May 1937, Barcelona experienced a tragic conflict between government forces and the anarchist Confederacion Nacional del Trabajo (CNT), a strong labor union that fought the Nationalist uprising and successfully collectivized land and industries. In the May days of 1937, a month before I was born, the CNT and its allies clashed with the Communist Party and the Republican government forces. They were forcefully evicted from their headquarters with tragic consequences: many died, and thousands were seriously wounded.

The revolution began to turn on itself.

*

Years later, I purchased a copy of *The New York Times* from the day I was born. I wanted to know what the world looked like on June 22, 1937, while my mother labored in that mountain village.

The reports were stark, almost clinical, but behind the words I recognized the fear. In the north, the paper noted that the destruction of bridges near Bilbao had slowed the Nationalist pursuit of the Basques. Exhausted loyalist forces were struggling to establish a new defensive line in the hills west of the city. Some had gone five days without sleep or food. In Madrid, a loyalist mine exploded under the Clinical Hospital in University City, killing hundreds of rebel soldiers. Loyalist troops intensified their push toward Huesca in northeastern Spain, trying desperately to offset the looming loss of Bilbao. At sea, an alleged submarine attack on the German cruiser Leipzig prompted protests from Berlin; the German foreign minister, Baron von Neurath, canceled a trip to London because other powers refused to punish "Loyalist Spain."

On the map, it appeared to be a strategy. On the ground, it was hunger, mud, shattered bone, and sleepless eyes. Children played among toppled statues, while men hunched in cafés over crumpled newspapers, their voices hoarse from arguments that never seemed to end. The country had not merely split along political lines, it had fractured along class, faith, and buried resentments.

In the wider world, 1937 kept adding its own catastrophes. Japan invaded China, marking the start of the Second Sino-Japanese War. In New Jersey, the German airship Hindenburg burst into flames and crashed, killing 36 and burning itself into the global imagination. Over the Pacific,

Amelia Earhart and her navigator, Fred Noonan, vanished while attempting to circumnavigate the globe. And in Paris, Pablo Picasso painted *Guernica*, his vast black-and-white scream of protest on canvas, after German planes bombed the Basque town of the same name. It was one of the first large-scale aerial massacres of civilians. Spain had become a warning to the world.

All of this happened in the year of my birth. While my mother held me in Gestalgar, history was throwing matches into barrels of gasoline.

I did not choose that moment or that place. But they shaped everything that followed.

The Spanish Civil War

Fascist Italy and Nazi Germany supported Franco in Spain by sending planes, tanks, weapons, and advisers. Fascist forces aimed to deploy a new warfare strategy called total obliteration, using Condor Legion bombers in repeated waves to reduce civilian-targeted cities to rubble. Britain and France, claiming neutrality, treated Spain as a distant issue, ignoring its implications for the impending European catastrophe. In Barcelona, the British consul cabled home with a revealing anxiety: "The government appears to be at the mercy of the workers."

The line reveals an old fear, not of violence or death, but of ordinary people gaining power and social equality. And yet, not everyone looked away.

Volunteers from the United States, Britain, Canada, and many other nations traveled in twos and threes by boat and train, crossing borders with little more than a backpack and a conviction: that Spain was fighting a battle that belonged to the conscience of the world. Many never returned. Idealism was not a metaphor then; it was something you carried on your shoulders, something you risked your life for.

Among those who refused to turn away was Dr. Norman Bethune, a Canadian surgeon who created a mobile blood transfusion service for the Republican forces. On the road from Málaga to Almería—during the exodus later known as La Desbandá—Bethune and his team tried to save civilians who were being bombed and strafed as they fled on foot: women holding infants, old men pushing carts, children stumbling beside them. In moments like that, war ceases to be ideology. It becomes dust in the lungs, blood on cloth, the raw terror of a road where the defenseless are treated as targets.

Another witness, the British journalist George Steer, walked into the ruins of Guernica and wrote plainly about what he saw. His dispatches helped the world understand what had happened — and reached Picasso, who turned that destruction into a black-and-white scream of protest that still refuses to quiet down. A bombed town became an image of the century.

Even among governments, a few showed moral clarity. Mexico stood openly with the Republic, a rare act of public courage amid the diplomatic evasions of the time.

And then there was Ernest Hemingway.

Hemingway did not fight as a soldier in Spain, but he did something nearly as consequential: he went as a witness. He traveled close enough to see the war's human texture — its courage, its fear, its betrayals, and its daily moral compromises. He also helped create a documentary in support of the Republic, *The Spanish Earth*, and narrated it in his own blunt voice, as if ornament itself might be a form of lying.

What Hemingway absorbed in Spain was not journalism. It became literature — an attempt to preserve not only events, but moral reality: what happens to ordinary men and women when history presses down on them with full weight.

That transformation culminated in *For Whom the Bell Tolls*. He chose as his central figure not a politician or a general, but a young American volunteer, Robert Jordan, working with guerrillas behind enemy lines. The mission is simple and impossible at once: destroy a bridge at the right moment, in the right way, amid confusion, shortage, mistrust, and fear. Everyone senses that the cause may already be lost.

Hemingway's genius was to show that even in a losing cause, dignity remains possible — that dignity is not a speech but a behavior. Loyalty. Steadfastness. The decision to do what must be done without demanding applause or certainty. His characters are not saints and not symbols; they are human beings — afraid, imperfect, sometimes petty, sometimes brave

— trying to act with coherence while the world fractures around them.

This is one of the Spanish Civil War's enduring lessons: history is not only a clash of ideologies; it is a trial of character.

The war, of course, was not morally clean on either side. Violence occurred in Republican zones as well — killings born of collapse, panic, revenge, and the breakdown of order. Clergy were among the victims, many of them posing no political threat. Yet a crucial distinction remains: the mass executions behind Nationalist lines known as the White Terror were not mere chaos. They were deliberate, organized, and encouraged from above, a political cleansing aligned with the logic of extermination rather than the fever of street violence.

And as if Spain needed one more tragedy, the Republic fractured from within. Barcelona became a warning inside the warning: a war within the war. Leftist factions turned against one another. Stalinist forces pursued purges; comrades became enemies; revolution bred informants. George Orwell, wounded and disillusioned, watched allies become jailers. What he carried out of Spain was not a partisan slogan but a hard-earned insight: authoritarianism is not the property of one ideology — it is a temptation of power itself.

Orwell later distilled that insight into two works that have stayed with me. *Animal Farm* begins as a dream of justice and ends in a familiar spectacle: rulers who resemble the tyrants they replaced. *1984* describes a state that does not merely control bodies but tries to colonize the mind through surveillance, propaganda, and the slow destruction of language itself. Orwell's vision did not come from theory alone. It came from seeing how quickly the machinery of fear can turn idealists into informants and comrades into wardens.

While I grew up under Franco, I never heard any of this.

We were taught a polished narrative: the Republic as chaos, the Nationalists as saviors, the nation rescued from disorder. Schoolbooks offered certainty, not complexity. Names were erased. Questions were discouraged. History was reduced to slogans. In Franco's Spain, facts were not merely difficult to find; they were dangerous. Even curiosity could feel like disloyalty.

Only later — after leaving Spain, after studying freely, after listening to voices long silenced — did I begin to grasp the depth of the tragedy. I learned what had been hidden: the organized killings, the moral contamination, the language of "cleansing," the ease with which extermination could be presented as national medicine. It felt as if I had walked through my own country with veiled eyes, breathing air filtered by fear.

In that belated awakening, Hemingway became more than a famous writer to me. He became a moral witness. His work offered a different education — one not aimed at obedience, but at clarity.

For Whom the Bell Tolls is not a perfect book, and Hemingway was not a perfect man. But the novel carries a harsh kind of mercy: it refuses to sentimentalize suffering, yet it does not surrender to cynicism. It insists that even when history becomes brutal, the soul is still tested — not by grand declarations, but by what you do when you are tired, frightened, compromised, and tempted to look away.

In that sense, the Spanish Civil War is not only history. It is a mirror. Movements often begin by claiming to protect the nation or the people. Then they demand silence, then loyalty, then worship. Tolerance becomes weakness. Pluralism becomes betrayal. Little by little, fear becomes policy. Spain learned this in blood. The world learned it soon after when Germany invaded Poland in 1939 triggering World War II.

Beneath the politics lies something more profound — something spiritual, though not sentimental. Hemingway understood that when death draws near, life comes into focus. His characters do not behave bravely because they believe in guaranteed victory. They behave bravely because they refuse to let despair define them. They accept that the cause may be lost, yet they act as if integrity still matters, because it does.

In Spain, in Hemingway's pages, and in Orwell's warnings, I see the same sober instruction: the world will test you — sometimes brutally. Yet, you are still responsible for the person you become.

That is the final gift the Spanish Civil War offers those of us who inherited its silence: not only knowledge of what happened, but a demand for inner clarity. We must refuse to waste our lives, and carry on to create a better world.

The Regime Evolves

On April 1, 1939, Franco declared, "The war is over." But, those of us who had survived knew better. The war had just changed disguises.

The Republic was crushed, and the country fell under the iron grip of Francisco Franco, who declared himself Caudillo *por la gracia de Dios* — by the grace of God. Spain slipped into a long, controlled darkness. Freedom itself was dismantled: political parties were banned, unions dissolved, newspapers reduced to obedient echoes of the regime, and Catalan and Basque languages prohibited.

Spain entered a second war marked by repression, intolerance, and silence, which was characterized mainly by acts of retribution. Life became colonized by fear. Post-war executions range from 50,000 to 100,000, depending on who counts and who dares to speak. The Law of Political Responsibilities allowed the regime to punish anyone who had ever supported the Republic, from ministers to village school-teachers.

Many more vanished into prisons and forced labor camps. Families, maimed by violence, learned to navigate a twisted moral landscape where words could condemn, whispers could betray, and silence was the only safe refuge.

Franco's regime erased the memory of many courageous heroes of the Republic such as Amparo Poch, and Dolores Ibárruri, La Pasionaria, whose defiant *"No pasarán!"* still echoes through Spain. Their names vanished from textbooks, their portraits disappeared from public buildings, and their stories survived only in whispers at kitchen tables.

There are wounds that time cannot heal. The Spanish Civil War left invisible scars — deep, silent fissures that continued to linger long after the gunfire stopped. In the way people paused before speaking. In the way they changed the subject when politics came up. I was born beneath that lingering shadow. When the bombs finally fell silent, Spain did not find peace. It simply entered a different kind of war: one without bullets but no less brutal. The repression was ruthless, and famine took hold. Spain was economically devastated. Agriculture failed; factories went quiet; food shortages arose.

In our home, we learned to survive with dignity and silence. Rationing was in place. Everyone was issued *cartillas de racionamiento*, small books that controlled what we could eat: a few ounces of flour, some rice if we were lucky, and a drop of oil. Meat was a distant dream, milk was a miracle, and sugar was a faint memory. We did not join the hundreds of thousands who fled to France, Mexico, or Argentina. We stayed.

Within the Valencian towns and villages, people felt safer and more connected when speaking our old language, Valencian/Catalan — the tongue once spoken in the Kingdom of Aragon. Words mattered. So did silence. We learned early to be cautious, to measure our words, and to keep our opinions private. Home was where we lowered our guard.

We survived with dignity wrapped in restraint. We trusted our neighbors, but never blindly. Caution became a form of intelligence. Silence, a shield.

We did not give in to despair.

Inside our Valencian world, warmth endured. It lived in humor shared behind closed doors, in loyalty tested over time, in food prepared the same way it had always been — paella without exception — and in wine mixed with *gaseosa*, poured from glass bottles held high above the head. You had to catch the stream midair, steady and precise, or miss it entirely. It was a small skill, but it mattered.

What sustained us was stubborn endurance. A quiet refusal to disappear. Even under pressure, even under watch, life insisted on continuing — through language, laughter, and shared tables. We learned that survival did not require surrender, only patience and the will to remain human.

*

In 1953, Spain signed agreements with the United States, trading five military bases on Spanish soil for financial and military aid. Anti-communism proved to be a powerful deterrent, helping to wash away the stain of fascist sympathies.

Franco's isolation ended when Dwight D. Eisenhower visited Spain in 1959. This was considered a form of rehabilitation for a regime that had been ostracized for supporting the Axis Powers during World War II. The regime was now a "strategic ally" of the Free World.

By the time I returned to Spain from America in the late 1960s to visit my family, the airports felt different. The Guardia Civil no longer barked commands like drill sergeants. There were fewer uniforms and more briefcases. The dictatorship had slipped into business suits.

Franco was old. People said, "Things are changing. It's better now." They weren't entirely wrong. They weren't entirely correct.

After Franco's death, things quickly changed, and Spain once again became a democracy. A parliamentary monarchy, that is, a social representative democratic constitutional monarchy, where the monarch is the head of state, and the prime minister, whose official title is "President of the Government," is the head of government. A government that, at least on paper, had checks and balances to prevent another Caudillo.

*

Looking back, the Second Republic seems both magnificent and doomed. It united various parties and ideologies: socialists, communists, anarchists, liberals, regional nationalists were all intoxicated with the idea of a new Spain. They fought for land reform, secular schools, dignity for workers, and women's emancipation. These changes were important; however, in their haste, they underestimated centuries of conservative Catholic tradition, the influence of wealthy landowners, and the emotional significance of old hierarchies.

Anti-clerical rage exploded. Churches were burned. Priests were shot. Conservative leaders like José Calvo Sotelo were assassinated. The other side responded with its own massacres. Justice and revenge bled into each other until you could barely tell them apart.

The beloved poet Federico García Lorca, who had given Spain some of its most luminous words, was murdered and dumped in an unmarked grave. His death is still one of the clearest symbols of a country killing its own soul.

I learned early that the Spanish Civil War was never just a Spanish affair. Even as a child, long before I could name ideologies, I sensed that what had happened around my birth was larger than our villages, larger than our grief. Spain had become a testing ground — a rehearsal for the great conflicts of the twentieth century: fascism against democracy, authoritarianism against freedom, force against conscience.

Those battles did not end with the war. They merely changed costumes.

I have watched their shadows return again and again, in different countries, under different flags. Yet I am also aware that the world we inhabit now is not that of the 1930s. History does not repeat itself cleanly. It mutates. The dangers today move faster, spread wider, and carry consequences that no border can contain.

Years ago, I came across a quote of Abraham Lincoln's that stayed with me: "The dogmas of the past are inadequate to the stormy present." I did not understand it fully when I first read it. I do now. What once served us can become an obstacle. Clinging to old answers in a changed world is not loyalty — it is folly.

What troubles me most today is not simply the return of old political reflexes, but the absence of vision. There is a vacuum where leadership should be. I see governments reacting rather than thinking, posturing rather than guiding.

I write this not as a politician or an ideologue, but as someone who has lived long enough to see what happens when societies lose their moral compass. I have seen what follows when short-term gain replaces long-term responsibility, when power is pursued without humility, when human lives become abstractions.

If there is a future worth defending, it will require a broader sense of responsibility — one that includes not only nations, but people everywhere; not only humans, but the living world that sustains us. No economic system can endure while ignoring the suffering it produces. No country can prosper in isolation while the ground beneath us — literal and moral — erodes.

The Pact of Forgetting

The question lingers: Who won the war?

For some, the answer is clear; the fascists did. They crushed the Republic and ruled for forty years. But ask someone else, and you might hear that Franco and the Nationalists "saved" the nation from Communism, sparing it from a Soviet-style dictatorship. Eight decades later, the Spanish Civil War remains an open wound of memory where no final truth prevails.

For forty years, the Franco regime imposed its own version of history. The Republic's cause was vilified, its ideals mocked, and its martyrs erased from history. Their bodies were buried under highways, in roadside ditches and in unmarked pits.

When the dictatorship finally ended in 1975, Spain made a decision: to move forward without fully looking back. The leaders of the transition, fearful of reopening old divisions, chose a policy of *el pacto del olvido* — the pact of forgetting. In 1977, the new parliament passed an Amnesty Law that effectively shielded Franco's officials from prosecution for war crimes. The hope was simple: if we don't reopen the wound, maybe it will heal. But the past is stubborn. These kinds of ghosts do not obey parliamentary decrees.

In the 2000s, families began to search for the remains of their loved ones. A quiet movement to recover historical memory took root. Judge Baltasar Garzón, already known for charging Chilean dictator Augusto Pinochet with crimes against humanity, turned his attention to Spain. In 2008, he opened an investigation into Franco-era atrocities, demanding that the fate of more than 130,000 disappeared Spaniards be clarified and that those responsible be held accountable.

For this act of courage, Garzón was not universally celebrated. He was sued, harassed, and eventually disbarred for eleven years by those who preferred silence. Yet, for many, he became a symbol of moral courage. In 2011, the Abraham Lincoln Brigade Archives in New York honored him with their first annual Human Rights Award.

The political divide remains. The center-right Popular Party (PP) argues that revisiting the past risks tearing open old wounds. The center-left Spanish Socialist Workers' Party (PSOE) insists that a mature democracy must face its history and confront its own crimes.

Stanley G. Payne, an American history professor at the University of Wisconsin and a prolific historian of modern Spain, has a more positive view of Franco, calling him "the most successful dictator of modern times." He wrote the book, *The Spanish Revolution,* and was appalled by what he discovered about the Spanish Second Republic. He says that the mass executions were as extensive as those carried out by Franco's supporters. Anticlericalism with its burnings of churches and slaughter of priests resulted in one of the greatest persecutions of Christians in modern times.

The truth is complicated. Every generation must decide how much truth it can bear.

Journalists Esperanza Escribano and Linda Presley delve into the history, legacy, and uncertain future of *El Valle de Cuelgamuros* — a site that continues to echo Spain's unresolved past.

Half a century after Francisco Franco's death, Spain is still searching for common ground between the opposing forces shaped by the Spanish Civil War. And no place captures those lingering tensions more vividly than the vast monument long known as *El Valle de los Caídos* — the Valley of the Fallen.

Constructed in part through the forced labor of political prisoners (one of my step-uncles was a prisoner there), the site was intended as a symbol of Franco's Nationalist triumph over Republican Spain. For decades, it became a pilgrimage site for his supporters — especially after Franco himself was buried behind the basilica's altar.

But in the twenty-first century, the country began to question the role of such memorials in a democratic society. Beginning in 2018, Spain's Socialist government sought to reshape the narrative. In 2019, Franco's remains were exhumed and removed from the site. It was then renamed *El Valle de Cuelgamuros*. And in 2025 — after difficult negotiations — plans were approved to transform the area into a space dedicated to democratic memory, rather than a monument glorifying dictatorship.

Yet the shift has not been universally welcomed. Some view it as historical revisionism, others as long-overdue justice. The debate continues, and the future of the Valley remains emblematic of Spain's ongoing struggle to reconcile its past.

*

The Spanish Civil War still matters because its lessons are loud in our own time.

The 1930s were an age of polarization, propaganda, and economic fear, whose reflection can be seen today. Democracies are especially vulnerable and need strong leadership that motivates and lifts their citizens. It's easy to sway the masses with propaganda for malicious purposes.

Now we live under hyper-capitalism, where anonymous corporations and oligarchs steer much of the world from glass towers. Disillusioned citizens, betrayed by inequality, listen again to voices offering simple answers — from the far right and from the far left. Socialism returns in new clothes, promising fairness and equality, but sometimes forgets its old temptation toward authoritarianism.

Watching Spain and later the United States, I learned that democracy is not a guarantee; it is a discipline that requires ongoing commitment. It depends on informed citizens, strong independent institutions, a free press, equal application of the law, protection for minorities, the capacity for compromise, and peaceful transfers of power.

Democracies rarely die with a single dramatic blow. They die slowly, as people grow tired, distracted, or afraid. They begin to forget.

And forgetting is always how it starts.

Returning to Gestalgar

For most of my life, Gestalgar was more a myth than a memory: a name on a birth certificate. When my mother fled to this tiny village while bombs rained from the skies of Valencia, my grandfather accompanied her. I know this not from photographs or stories, but because his name appears beside hers on my birth certificate as a witness to my arrival in the world.

I hadn't set foot in Gestalgar until recently. Over the years, I spoke to city hall clerks many times to request official documents, always promising myself that someday I would go. But "someday" tends to slip away unless we make it part of a plan. In 2023 that plan finally came together.

I needed another copy of my birth certificate, this time to fulfill a bureaucratic requirement at the police station in Valencia so I could finally get my Spanish passport. Although I had regained my Spanish citizenship at the consulate in Miami after many years abroad, the last step required a visit to my hometown.

Juanjo, a cousin from Valencia, offered to drive my wife and I. Jovial, generous, and always full of energy, Juanjo picked us up in his sleek Porsche. He drove along winding roads until the small village of Gestalgar gradually appeared, surrounded by rolling hills, lush greenery, and the Turia River. The church tower stood out prominently, and El Castillo, an historic landmark on a hill overlooking the town, hinted at a forgotten noble lord from a medieval story.

"Can you manage to drive through these tiny streets, designed for donkeys rather than Porsches?" I asked Juanjo.

"Of course, donkeys never had this power."

He drove smoothly through the uneven cobblestone streets of the village. We passed a café where locals sat outside. He crossed the town and parked near the River Turia, the same river that once flowed through the city of Valencia.

The village felt timeless, quiet, and still. Locals, who never seemed to feel hurried, filled the outdoor tables of the single café where life revolved. They sipped their coffees slowly, talked, and watched the day pass by like clouds drifting across the sky. It was as if the rest of the world didn't matter here.

We parked near a stream that traced a silver line around the village. Off in the distance stood the rock formations of *Peña Maria* and the crumbling ruins of *El Castillo*.

After immersing myself back into the past, I turned to the practical matter that had brought me here. The town hall wasn't hard to find. It was right in the center of town. I entered with a mix of anticipation and reverence, as if I were stepping into the room where my existence was first documented.

To my surprise, the city clerks were young, articulate, and warm. They welcomed me as a long-lost son of the village. One of them even handed me a book written by a fellow native of Gestalgar. We talked, laughed, and shook hands. I committed to sending them a copy of my memoir upon its publication.

With my newly printed birth certificate in hand, I returned to Valencia and made my way to the police station. After a bit of waiting, *voilà!* I was handed my Spanish passport and ID card.

I am now officially a dual citizen: one foot in the Old World, one in the New. Spain has a rich, complex history as a country that once explored the unknown, conquered empires, and stuck to tradition and the Catholic Church for centuries. My other foot is firmly planted in the United States, a land of bold ideas, a utopian revolution rooted in Enlightenment philosophy and the courage to create a constitution that promised liberty and justice for all when monarchy was the only political system imaginable.

These two worlds haven't always matched up, but they now coexist within me. Standing at this intersection of cultures has taught me that no country, no people, and no identity are complete. Everything is dynamic and keeps changing. There is still a lot of work to do on both sides of the ocean. Progress can easily be reversed if we're not careful.

I see how deeply Spain influenced me, not only through my memories but by shaping my values. It is a land brimming with beauty, warmth, and effortless human connections, where conservative ideas and traditional religious and social values now coexist harmoniously with progressive ones. Spain gave me a beautiful, expressive language, rhythm, and a deep respect for family and tradition.

Spain is no longer the country I left. When it joined the European Communities, the precursor to the European Union, on January 1, 1986, the transformation began in earnest. But the bigger change had already been set in motion years earlier, in the determined transition to democracy that followed Franco's death. Watching Spain learn to stand alongside other European nations, to cooperate, to innovate, and to compete on equal terms filled me with pride. The long era of isolation had finally ended, and a new chapter for the peninsula had begun.

Each time I return — whether to Madrid, Valencia, Seville, or Barcelona — I sense that change not only in the architecture and the rhythms of the streets, but in the voices of the newcomers who now call Spain home. Taxi drivers from Latin America often share their stories with me and the refrain is the same: they feel safe, welcome, and able to build a life with dignity. Their contentment speaks volumes. Spain has become a land of opportunity, a place where immigrants feel they can breathe and plan for a future.

Elma Saiz, Spain's Minister of Inclusion, Social Security, and Migration, recently said that Spain has become "a beacon." I believe her. The country I once left in search of freedom is now attracting others seeking the same. Due to the harsh anti-immigrant policies of the Trump administration, many who once dreamed of the United States are now looking to Spain. Seeing my homeland evolve into a place of refuge and opportunity brings me great joy. It shows what a nation can become when it chooses democracy, openness, and compassion.

Chapter 2: Early Years

"All that I am, or ever hope to be, I owe to my angel mother."

–Abraham Lincoln

The Motherless Child

I was five when it happened. Our mother died suddenly without explanation. One morning we had a mother, and the next, we didn't. My older brother and I were left with an ache we couldn't name. To this day, I don't know what took her.

My last memory of her was playing with my brother. I watched two kids jumping up and down on the master's bedroom mattress, filled with envy. I could see her protruding belly. She was happy and pregnant. Her vanishing didn't just leave a hole; it rearranged the entire map of my world. We were too young to understand grief but not too young to feel the disorientation of being motherless, untethered from the one person whose love was unwavering.

For a while, we stayed with our aunt, my father's sister, in Mislata. She had daughters of her own, Finin and Carmencin, who were older than us so we didn't play with them too often. Still, we were welcomed into that house, and we adjusted.

I remember days when we enjoyed paella, the traditional Valencian rice dish, accompanied by tasty pieces of chicken, rabbit, pork, and seafood. We all sat around the dining room table with the large, shallow pan, where the meal was cooked and placed right in the middle of the round table. Using our wooden spoons, each of us scooped from the edges toward the center. Occasionally I found lots of meat and seafood pieces and other times fewer, but I always looked forward to eating the crispy rice layer at the bottom of the pan, known as "*socarrat*" in the Valencian dialect.

My dad used to visit us on Saturdays to enjoy the special paella my aunt made for him. When I found him alone, I would ask for a dime to buy candy. He had a limited vocabulary. I worried that one day he might say no. That would have been devastating and humiliating, but he never did. This was my secret connection with him, which felt caring.

We enjoyed hot, juicy sandwiches straight from the oven for dinner, then went outside to play after we ate. This was our evening routine. However, my brother and I felt like passengers in someone else's life. We knew we were in transition, waiting for something. Waiting for what? We didn't know.

One day, my father returned but this time he didn't come alone; he brought Amelia.

She was from the big city, Madrid, the capital of Spain. It showed in her shoulder slope, her clothes, the precision of her speech, and the way she wore elegance like armor. She was beautiful, but in a way that felt slightly aloof and dangerous. She smiled with restraint, the kind that suggested you shouldn't assume too much. But she brought us gifts and comic books and I clutched mine as if it were a ticket to somewhere better.

A few days later, we moved again, this time to Alacuàs, back to the same house where we had once lived with our mother. My mother's presence still lingered in the dust and light: the angle of the sun shining through the kitchen window, the silence in the room where her voice used to be. The house remembered, even if the grown-ups preferred to act otherwise. Now, there was a new woman in the house. She was quiet and said little at first.

Then came the afternoon that divided what came before from what came after. Amelia called a meeting.

That's how I remember it, formal, serious, as if we'd been summoned to explain ourselves. She stood at the head of the dining table, the same table that once held birthday cakes and Sunday dinners. It looked enormous to me then, as if grief had carved out that space between us.

She cleared her throat and announced the news plainly. "I've spoken with your father," she said. "We've decided that I won't be raising you boys."

No preamble. No apology. The clarity of a decision already made is all that's needed. She was not accepting us as her children; she was building a barrier between us and herself.

Her voice was steady, but the room felt frozen. I turned to my brother, older and usually calm, and saw tears in his eyes. That frightened me more than the words themselves. I had never seen him cry like that.

"Stop crying," I told him sharply and instinctively. "We don't need her. We'll take care of ourselves."

Inside, I was unraveling in shock. Her rejection hit me like a sudden poison. I didn't yet know how to mourn something that had never fully been offered: her protection, her future with us. What hurt most wasn't her refusal, it was her certainty. She could have allowed the silence to convey its own message. Instead, she made it official by saying it clearly and aloud.

That day marked a deep emotional change within me, affecting not just my childhood but also the very core of my inner life. I started building walls, hidden yet effective, designed to keep disappointment away. If the promise of love could be taken away so easily, I would learn not to rely on it. If care could disappear overnight, I would learn to depend on myself, and I did. That self-reliance became my guiding principle throughout my life. I became a traveler, not only across countries but also within myself.

Over time, I recognized something more intricate. Amelia wasn't unkind. She was cautious with her affection and firm with her boundaries. But she believed in one thing with great passion: education. She pushed us, not gently, not tenderly, but with the force of someone who had seen enough of the world to understand how narrow it could be. Without her insistence, I might have stayed in that small town outside Valencia. I might never have studied medicine, never crossed an ocean, never stood at the bedside of strangers, and never learned, moment by moment, how to piece them (and myself) back together.

She was not heartless; she lacked the awareness that some things are better left unsaid. She didn't understand how her words affected her stepchildren or that she had already committed to caring for us when she married our father. Her awkward attempt to take back part of that decision wasn't well thought out. She couldn't undo it, we were there, she was there, and no one was going anywhere. In the end, she took excellent care of us and everything else. She just needed to express her mixed feelings openly.

If I had been an adult with the right words, I might have reassured her that she shouldn't be afraid of us, that we wouldn't cause her much trouble, and that she shouldn't doubt her maternal instincts. She did have them, and she proved it abundantly in the years that followed.

Back then, none of that mattered. All I knew was we were on our own. I told myself we could survive. I believed that I didn't need much from anyone, and I repeated this for decades. It became my creed, my armor.

Low expectations, I thought, were the key to a life without disappointments. However, with age, perhaps softened by time, I've come to understand what I couldn't before: being on your own isn't the same as being alone. The walls you build to keep pain out also keep love from coming in. And that boy at the table, the one who told his brother to stop crying, was trying to feel stronger by building his shield and denying his pain. He was just starting the long journey.

The Toy Factory

When the dust had settled from the war but the fear hadn't, my father and grandfather did something quietly radical: they decided to make toys.

They founded *Juguetes Mediterráneos.*

Music ran in our blood. My great-grandfather and grandfather had crafted accordions; my grandfather, a composer who could silence a plaza with a single raised hand, directed the Mislata orchestra. They built musical toys — small machines of joy. Turn a handle, and a melody appeared. In the gray monotony of Franco's Spain, they manufactured color and sound.

My father became one of the leading employers in Alacuás. Many of his workers were former comrades from the Republican front. They had lost a country but found work among friends who remembered where they had stood when it mattered. In a dictatorship that wanted obedient workers and quiet children, our family made objects that played, sang, and moved. It was a modest rebellion in the key of C major.

The first factory took shape inside my Aunt Fina's house in Mislata. It wasn't much, just a modest home watched over by two ancient trees that no one ever watered, yet they always lived. Down a cool corridor, you'd find a room of long tables where men and women assembled toys by hand: flutes, drums, pianos, harmonicas, little accordions, returning music to a country still mourning itself.

One of the factory workers, a man named Messeger, took it upon himself to teach me communism, though I was far too young to absorb the ideology. I could feel how painful it was for him to see his dreams turn to ash when the war was lost.

Every summer, I worked at the factory. I protested, but it felt like going to summer camp, and at least I was near my father and learned a lot from interacting with the workers. That was better than staying home.

My father's business partner, Ferrero, handled national sales. He was slick, persuasive. Ferrero once interviewed me as a potential heir to the factory. I answered his questions with deliberate foolishness. I had no intention of inheriting a business that imprisoned its owners. My brother, more dutiful, took up the mantle. He endured the long commutes and tried to live up to their expectations. But eventually, even he cracked.

When he asked for a motorcycle and was told no, he left for Paris in search of air that didn't come with tram delays and unrewarding duty. My father, confused and heartbroken, never understood that the real betrayal wasn't my brother's departure, it was the rigidity of the life and world he was trying to preserve.

The factory moved again, this time to Aldaya. My father brought on a younger partner, full of ambition, but slowly, the dream unraveled. The toy factory, once a symbol of resilience, became my father's cage. He couldn't leave it. Loyalty held him there long after joy had gone.

In the end, it wasn't business alone that undid him, it was medicine, too. He died within the folds of a fragmented, bureaucratic, incompetent health system. I lived in the United States when he had a hernia repair; complications followed. I tried to save him, but everything seemed to be stacked against us.

There are many ways to lose your freedom. Some prisons have walls. Others are built out of silence, duty, and denial. You don't always see them until the door has quietly closed behind you.

I learned from the factory that we must choose our partnerships wisely, in business, in medicine, and in love. And we must always leave room for movement, music, and retreat when the situation turns into a trap.

My brother escaped. I escaped. My father did not.

La Madrileña

The phone rang twice before I heard his voice pick up on the other end of the line.

"*¡Hermano!* How's life treating you?" Pepe boomed warmly.

"Pepe!" I smiled foolishly into the receiver, "Finally! I thought you'd forgotten I existed. I'm persevering, but nowhere near as creative as you. You're still painting, writing, and posting your little masterpieces online. You are a true celebrity. I envy you, bro."

He barked a laugh. "Celebrity? Please. You're the one saving people's minds and lives. I just splash paint around and rant on TikTok." That was Pepe, always generous, sneaking in compliments.

"So, tell me," I asked, "how's Madrid?"

"It's still Madrid," he said. "Loud, chaotic, and irresistible. The traffic honks in a symphony, the *terrazas* smell of garlic and wine, and somehow, I ended up in the same city Amelia came from. Dad's family always called her *la madrileña*."

I chuckled. "And she never shook the title, even after decades in Valencia. I've been thinking about her a lot lately."

"Why now?" he asked.

"Good question. For years, I painted her as the villain in my story. But time's a strange magician, it shifts the light and shows you new angles. Now I see her more clearly."

We both remembered her panic attacks whenever Dad was late for lunch from the toy factory. She'd sit at the table trembling, tears welling, convinced he'd died in some accident. No amount of reason calmed her, only his face at the door did. At the time, I found it maddening. Now I see it as love. Love spoken in the language of fear of loss, fear of abandonment.

Pepe chuckled. "She was dramatic, yes. But strong too."

"Strong? Oh yes. Remember when she moved in and told us, cold as a marble statue, 'I'm not going to raise you.'"

Pepe's voice softened, "You told me, but I don't remember it."

"Well, I remember this: you saving my life in the *acequia* of Mislata."

He laughed. "Ah, so you do admit it! You were flailing like a frog in a blender. I grabbed you before the stream carried you off to Valencia."

He was right, I owed him more than I could ever say.

Silence stretched between us, not awkward, but a warmth.

"You know," I said, "Amelia was a storm. Fierce, unpredictable. But storms clear the air. When she opened that clothing shop with her friend, she came alive. She was laughing, radiant, and confident. She had potential but being stuck as a housewife soured her. I think she resented us, not for what we did, but for reminding her we weren't hers."

"She never let us forget it either," Pepe said quietly.

"No. She carried that wound to the grave. But she did care. Fiercely. In her own emotional way."

After we hung up, I thought about how Amelia and my father shared a life of routine that neither of them knew how to escape. How both endured roles they did not choose. I saw how much she loved and how deeply she feared rejection and abandonment.

There was one memory that belonged more to Pepe than to me. When he finished middle school, the director had pocketed the money meant to register students for the official exam. Most children were excluded. Their futures stalled.

Amelia went straight to the school. She confronted the man. No hesitation. No fear.

Miraculously, Pepe's name appeared on the list. He took the exam. He passed. He moved forward.

I don't know what happened to the others. I only know they didn't have Amelia. She was fire. Too much fire for a small house. And I, younger and angrier, saw only the flames. I turned inward. I leaned on Pepe.

She accused us often. "You don't love me because I'm not your real mother."

We denied it. We insisted. But she never believed us. She expected rejection and lived inside that expectation.

Amelia, I know you are gone now. I was there at your hospital bed and held your hand when you took your last breath. For years I mistook your worry for control. Your toughness for cruelty. Now I know better.

You were there. You showed up. You took care of us when we were fragile and had no say in our lives. After the war, when you came into our lives, you showed caring and skills that no woman in our village had. You made clothes and sandals for us from scratch, from whatever materials you could find. You dressed us like we were little princes in a world of scarcity.

Sometimes presence is love, even when it comes wrapped in sharp words.

I never said it when it mattered. I say it now.

Thank you for staying. For caring. For protecting us in the only ways you knew how. I was quick to judge. Slow to understand. I didn't know then that adults are still learning how to love while fearing abandonment. That family love does not always speak softly.

Now, with more road behind me than ahead, I carry your memory without anger. If these words reach you in any way, let them be simple. I'm sorry. And thank you.

The Curious Teen

We think of morality as carved in stone, as the Ten Commandments supposedly were. We believe that those rules should apply to everyone, everywhere. Any violation of those rules should bring the inevitable just punishment. So, when I was young, that's what I believed.

My teenage years were spent growing up in strict, puritanical Catholic Spain. Sex was considered taboo, something that shouldn't be discussed or even mentioned in the morally upright Spanish family. However, hormones inevitably develop in teenagers' bodies, both boys and girls.

These hormones play a crucial role by nourishing and transforming every cell, including those in the brain, muscles, hair, breasts, and genitals, and they shape the way that boys and girls present themselves to the outside world. This is nature, and there's nothing you can say or do to change it. It simply happens. The hormones exist for a purpose, and their purpose is reproduction. Hormones are unaware of chastity or the morality of a culture. All of this occurs unknowingly to the unsuspecting teenager.

After our time in Mislata and Alacuás, my brother and I lived with my father and step-mother in an apartment in Valencia. Amelia was used to having domestic help, like most middle-class Spanish women do. Young women usually provided this help. These girls came from impoverished rural areas with limited employment opportunities and few prospects for young people. As a result, they moved to the cities, offering their skills in cooking and cleaning; sometimes they also cared for children and the elderly.

At this time, we had an unusually young domestic helper. She lived with us and had her own room. Fortune had it that her room was right across from ours, where Pepe and I slept in separate beds. Our parents went out at night quite often, leaving the three of us alone. At first, I thought nothing of it until I began noticing that my brother was getting up at night and frequently looking out the window. I was intrigued; I got up, and to my horror, he was watching a strip show. The girl was teasing my brother by dressing and undressing in her nightgown. I thought that what was happening was wrong, and I feared my brother would get in trouble. Trouble arrived faster than I expected. The watching soon turned into nocturnal visits.

I didn't say anything, so I didn't think my parents would ever know what was going on after they left to go to the movies or socialize.

Before long, something happened. The girl couldn't help herself and started talking carelessly and indiscreetly about having an affair with *el señorito*. She told everyone she met, the clerks at the grocery store, the butcher's shop, and everywhere she bought groceries and household items. Some of the clerks knew my stepmother and got worried. They thought my father was responsible. They told my stepmother, who then went into a frenzy. She confronted my father, who claimed he was innocent. Then they discovered there was another *señorito* in the house: my brother. They confronted him, and he admitted it. The girl was fired and sent back to her village. My father confronted my brother and, to my surprise, told him to leave the help alone and that if he needed relief, he would take him to a brothel. Brothels were a common, licensed, and accepted business in Franco's Spain until Spain joined the United Nations.

What struck me most was not the act itself, but the response.

Rather than being punished, my brother was rewarded. Not formally, of course, but clearly enough. A discreet arrangement was made. A prepaid visit to a brothel. No drama. No sermon. Adults simply nodded and understood each other.

Sex, it seemed, was not such a terrible thing after all. You just had to do it the right way. With the right woman, or at least in the right place.

My brother accepted the offer without hesitation.

At the time, I did not know how to approach or think about the issue, but it stayed with me. It taught me something important, though not what the adults intended. I learned that grown-ups were far more flexible than their rules suggested. Public morality and private behavior lived in different rooms. What was condemned in words was often tolerated, even facilitated, in practice.

Compared to my brother and most of my peers, I was a prude. I knew it then. I feel it even more clearly now. I don't fully know why. But I suspect it had something to do with how early I developed a rigid moral compass — and how deeply I worried about causing harm to others, especially women.

I had absorbed the message of my culture, at that time and place: sex was supposed to belong to love, or at least to commitment. Outside of marriage, it was framed as wrong. Dangerous. It was viewed as a source of shame. Casual sex was not just discouraged; it was morally unacceptable. I didn't know then that over time, those norms change.

No one explained how to reconcile desire with decency. Or how to want without shame. Or how to be honest about longing without feeling morally defective. The result was confusion: desire was natural and expected. Acting on it was not. Guilt and remorse had to be overcome if you dared to go outside the established norms.

I was too young. So I learned to wait. To restrain myself.

Sex and desire are awkward subjects. They expose the tension between instinct and conscience, between what the body wants and what the mind has been taught to fear. I did not resolve that tension at the time. It followed me across borders and years.

Juan Luis Vives: A Renaissance Sage from Valencia

Long after I left Spain, certain names from my youth began to resonate with new significance. My high school in Valencia, Spain, was named after a man I scarcely knew as a teenager: Juan Luis Vives March, a Renaissance scholar from my hometown. The official name was El Instituto Luis Vives. The name of my high school started to symbolize much more than I initially realized. It wasn't just a building or a school; it was a silent thread connecting me to a man whose story, when I finally uncovered it, felt strangely familiar. In Juan Luis Vives, I found not only a fellow exile but also a kindred spirit who had walked the same streets of Valencia centuries before and who, like me, had sought intellectual freedom in lands far from home.

This was a public school, supposedly secular, unlike many Catholic schools run by priests, Jesuits, and monastic orders. I thought it would be my refuge from the overwhelming influence of religious indoctrination that had permeated Spanish education for centuries. In those schools, the Jesuit motto: *Las letras con sangre entran* — "To learn, draw blood"— captured the spirit of that era. I had already experienced my share of those religious schools that couldn't understand.

The walls of the grand old building were covered with beautiful blue tiles, and the attached church whose basement was used as a burial site for long-dead priests and nuns. That building held my youthful years of struggle, rebellion, and silent protest of a system that seemed determined to break our spirits.

But even in the public secular school, we were forced to attend a mandatory Mass every morning before classes. They had a system by which the gates and all doors would be locked before Mass ended. If the students were not inside the church by the end of Mass, they could not attend classes.

I thought that was wrong, unjust. Nobody should be forced to attend a religious event, that should be voluntary. Eventually, my rebellion and my new faith caused me to skip the mandatory Mass, which got me into trouble. I had secretly joined an illegal Protestant church, a risky act under Franco's regime, where Catholicism was the only officially approved faith.

Some days, when caught hiding in the bathrooms, I would be suspended from school and wander the streets of Valencia — a lonely teenage truant wrestling with questions bigger than himself.

Amid this darkness, the Institute offered me glimpses of light. A few teachers genuinely cared about their students. An Anglophile English teacher, Señor Carreres, styled himself like a British dandy and brought a breath of fresh air to the classroom. A literature teacher, Señora Carol, nurtured my passion for forbidden classics, allowing me to read such works as *La Celestina* and *The Decameron*. Even the eccentric math teacher, who scrawled indecipherable equations on the blackboard while muttering to himself in ecstasy, remains a quirky but endearing memory. The director who taught philosophy and whose loyalty to the regime got him the job was an interesting man. He was a devout Catholic who didn't believe in contraceptives. He had twelve children and counting at the time. They all would parade together to find their seats in the auditorium when foreign films were shown. They reminded me of the children from the Trapp family featured in *The Sound of Music*.

The strange thing was that, despite the name of Juan Luis Vives on the building, I knew almost nothing about the man. It wasn't until much later in my life, as an adult living in exile myself, that I finally discovered things about the scholar who now feels like a kindred spirit across centuries.

Juan Luis Vives was born in Valencia on March 6, 1493 — just a year after the Catholic Monarchs expelled all Jews from Spain. He was born into a family of conversos, Sephardic Jews who converted to Catholicism in a desperate attempt to survive increasing persecution. The Inquisition was relentless, driven by greed as much as piety. Converting wasn't enough; conversos were constantly monitored and accused of secretly practicing Judaism. Many continued to cling to their ancestral traditions in secret.

Vives' father, Luis Vives Valeriola, was first prosecuted for Judaizing in 1477 and was later burned at the stake in 1524 after a second trial. His mother, Blanquina March, converted in 1491 to protect the family but died during a plague in 1508. Even after her death, the Inquisition exhumed her remains twenty years later and publicly burned her body as punishment for alleged secret visits to the synagogue.

What kind of men dig up the dead to burn their bones? What kind of mental cruelty wears the robes of the Church?

I suspect that greedily taking the financial assets of the victims for the church may have often been behind the accusations.

It's staggering to grasp that Vives lived and wrote while these horrors engulfed his family. As his loved ones were tortured and executed, Juan Luis, only sixteen, fled Spain for Paris in 1509. He would never return. Like me, centuries later, he left behind a homeland infected by religious extremism and intolerance, a land that could not tolerate difference, diversity, or dissent.

From exile, Vives flourished into one of the greatest minds of his time. He moved through the leading intellectual circles of Europe: Paris, Louvain, Bruges, and the court of Henry VIII in England, where he tutored Princess Mary and befriended Thomas More. Erasmus admired him greatly. More declared he would "eclipse Erasmus himself."

He published works of astonishing modernity, including the books: *On the Education of a Christian Woman*, advocating education for women, which was a radical idea at the time; *On Assistance to the Poor*, envisioning state-supported welfare systems; *On Concord and Discord in Humankind*, condemning war and exalting peace; and *This Course Provides an Introduction to Wisdom*, blending Stoic philosophy with Christian ethics.

As a social reformer, ethicist, and early psychologist, Vives denounced scholasticism's sterile logic and emphasized the complexity of human emotion, education, and memory.

Psychiatric historian Gregory Zilboorg even called him "the godfather of psychoanalysis."

But his courage came at a cost. He dared to support Queen Catherine of Aragon against Henry VIII's divorce — a brave but dangerous act. The king placed him under house arrest. Eventually, Vives returned to Bruges, where he married and died in 1540 at the age of 47.

The tragedy of his family haunts me: how much suffering they endured simply for being different. And how much Spain lost because of its blind fanaticism. The Sephardic Jews had been the doctors, bankers, merchants, and scholars — the backbone of intellectual and economic life. Even Luis de Santángel, a converso financier from Valencia, was instrumental in funding Columbus's voyage in 1492. But once Spain purged its Jewish and Muslim populations, it entered centuries of decline, marked by poverty, illiteracy, incompetent monarchs, and endless religious wars.

The Inquisition, a brutal instrument of cruelty, persisted until it was officially abolished in 1834. The Jesuits were also expelled during the reign of Bourbon reformer King Carlos III, who saw the harmful partnership between the Church and the State.

Spain, once a beacon of tolerance under Muslim rule — with its thriving coexistence of Christians, Jews, and Muslims — fell apart under the weight of its prejudice. The

Golden Age did not end because of foreign enemies but because of internal ideological intolerance.

Even today, Spain tries to make amends, offering citizenship to descendants of Sephardic Jews. Some of my Jewish friends have accepted this offer and are symbolically returning to the land their ancestors had to flee. The gesture feels sincere but centuries too late.

What lessons can we learn from this? That enforced unity, whether religious, ethnic, or ideological, inevitably breeds intolerance. In contrast, diversity is strength. It enriches cultures, arts, science, and economies.

The wisdom of the American Founders in separating church and state remains one of the most enlightened achievements of modern civilization. Yet even here, religious groups try to infiltrate public education, pushing non-Christians to the margins.

The story of Juan Luis Vives isn't just about one man, it's about many self-exiled wanderers. I don't compare myself to his intellectual achievements during the Renaissance, only in very superficial ways. Like him, I left Spain during Franco's rule, disillusioned by authoritarianism and a Church that still claimed control over minds and souls. Like him, I sought freedom of thought in foreign countries.

Vives achieved success despite facing numerous challenges. He reminds me that tolerance, compassion, and the life of the mind will always outshine the small, bitter men who persecute others in the name of God.

Someday, I hope, Juan Luis Vives' dream will come true: a world free of needless wars, governed by reason and peace.

In rediscovering Vives, I learned more about myself, not just as a doctor or an exile, but as part of a lineage of dissenters who refused to conform to their society's norms and authorities. When you join another community with values more aligned with yours, you regain a sense of normalcy. His story reminded me that self-exile, while painful, can also be a clarifying experience. It removes illusions, sharpens convictions, and reveals what truly matters. Like Vives, I left behind a country that tried to silence differences. And like him, I chose a life rooted not in obedience but in inquiry, compassion, and the enduring belief that the mind must stay free.

Chapter 3:
At the Crossroads

"It is not our abilities that show what we truly are; it is our choices."

—J.K. Rowling

Forging a Moral Compass

The year after I completed my *Baccalauréat* (Spain's equivalent to high school) I was unsure about what to do with my life. As I approached adulthood after completing my studies in Valencia, the burden of choices became more pressing. The world before me was a maze of expectations, illuminated only a few steps ahead, with the destination still hidden.

Medicine terrified me. It felt vast, almost holy. The textbooks of medical students looked impossibly thick, as if they required memorizing the entire human body. But beneath that fear, there was a voice that spoke not of titles nor riches but of service.

The foundation of my moral compass began to form through watching life around me, reading stories, and watching movies. It really gelled after high school, when I began thinking about my future, deciding what I wanted to be and how to go about it. I was certain that I needed to create a purposeful life, one that would add meaning while also providing a livelihood. I remember making a deliberate decision to be helpful and to not harm others. There are moments in life that arrive without fanfare, quiet and unannounced, when one gradually becomes aware that something invisible is forming inside.

Like the old seamen crossing vast waters, who held their magnetic compasses close to their chests, I, too, would one day come to rely on an inner device to navigate life's uncertain terrain. This compass did not shout, argue, or seek to impress. It whispered.

I realized that a moral compass is not something you are born with fully formed. It develops over time, shaped by many influences: family, teachers, books, failures, strangers. Education smooths it out. Suffering engraves it. Compassion lubricates its hidden gears. But above all, reflection, the quiet work of honest self-examination, adjusts it.

Without a clear guiding principle, it's easy to drift into the tempting waters of convenience, succumbing to immediate pleasures that deceive you and justify choices that benefit oneself while harming others. I've known men like this, bright and ambitious but lost. They confuse cleverness with wisdom, ruthlessness with leadership, and ambition with virtue. They rise quickly but leave a trail of destruction behind. The corporate world is full of men like that.

This is what Hieronymus Bosch conveys through his masterful, allegorical paintings. Your life's journey is filled with temptations, and you might fall for them, but remember, God is watching. Ultimately, you will be held accountable for your actions. I believe a moral compass works the same way as Christ overseeing the traveler. If you follow the right path, the reward may not be a vague, undefined Heaven, but it could be found in enjoying a happy and healthy life in this world surrounded by good friends and family and experiencing the fulfillment that comes from living your life true to your purpose.

Lessons from Four Films

Two films from my childhood helped forge my moral compass long before I knew what ethics meant. *Pinocchio* and *The Wizard of Oz* are two stories that spoke to the heart of a child but carried truths intended for a lifetime.

Carlo Collodi's *The Adventures of Pinocchio* enchanted me the moment I saw that wooden puppet come to life, full of curiosity, temptation, and mischief. Like every child, I recognized something of myself in him. I saw the impulse to follow the easiest path, the lure of pleasure over responsibility, and the foolish belief that we can deceive others without consequence.

Pinocchio's growing nose was not just a clever trick; it was a symbol of conscience made visible. The Talking Cricket, who tried again and again to warn and guide Pinocchio on the right path, became more than just a character to me. It transformed into the voice of foresight and moral awareness.

As a boy, I learned from Pinocchio that choices matter. That following bad advice leads us astray. That it is essential to listen to one's conscience (our inner "cricket") to stay human in a world that constantly tempts us to become something less. Foresight, I later realized, is the true heart of morality: the ability to imagine the consequences of one's actions before they unfold.

My own "Talking Cricket" would later take the form of intuition, hesitation, or doubt whispering in the back of my mind before a crucial decision.

Another moral revelation came from *The Wizard of Oz*. A glorious technicolor dream of courage, friendship, and the quest for home. Dorothy, Toto, and her unlikely companions of the Scarecrow, the Tin Man, and the Cowardly Lion taught me that what we seek is often already within us. The journey itself, not the destination, is what awakens the strength we doubt we possess.

What struck me most deeply as a child was not the flying monkeys or the wicked witches, it was the Wizard himself. The Great and Powerful Oz — who thundered from behind a screen, commanding fear and reverence was finally revealed to be just an ordinary man pulling levers and speaking into a microphone.

That moment opened my eyes to the fact that authority, despite its appearance of spectacle and noise, is not always truthful. Behind many grand voices and glowing screens, there may be only fragile men pretending to be gods. From *The Wizard of Oz*, I learned to not be afraid of power or appearances. It instilled in me a lifelong skepticism towards arrogant authority, be it political, religious, or scientific, and a determination to scrutinize the details before accepting anything.

In time, I would come to see the film's more profound allegory: the Yellow Brick Road as the Gold Standard, the Emerald City as the illusion of paper wealth, and Dorothy as the innocent American spirit led astray by false promises. But even as a child, before I could grasp its economic symbolism, I understood its moral one. The film taught me that the wizard does not bestow courage, love, and intelligence; they must be discovered within ourselves.

Together, *Pinocchio* and *The Wizard of Oz*, constituted the two pillars of my moral compass: inner honesty and outer courage. Those early lessons became the foundation for the choices that would follow: the crossroads of youth, the profession I would choose, and the voice I would one day learn to trust.

Two other movies significantly changed my understanding of people's perspectives on reality, truth, and justice when I was a young man.

I first encountered *Rashomon* in Spain in 1951, not long after its release. The cinema was small, the seats creaked, and the air smelled faintly of tobacco and damp wool coats. I was still young yet already restless, searching for something in stories that would explain the contradictions I saw in the world around me. Kurosawa's masterpiece had a profound impact on me.

On the screen, a torrential rainstorm poured over the ruined Rashomon gate. Under its dripping eaves, desperate men sheltered, each recounting what they had seen (or claimed to have seen) of a murder in the forest. A bandit, a wife, a dead husband speaking through a medium, and a passing woodcutter all told the same story, yet none of their versions matched. Every detail each witness recounted contradicted the previous one defending his or her honor. Each version became more self-serving than the last.

I remember whispering to my brother as the credits rolled, "But who do you believe?"

He shrugged, his eyes still fixed on the blank screen. "Maybe none of them. Maybe all of them."

That was the brilliance of Kurosawa. He forced me to confront a reality I had sensed but never expressed; reality is elusive and subjective. Each of us holds on to a story that preserves our self-image. We distort, we embellish, and we forget, sometimes without even realizing it.

That realization transformed me. It taught me patience with people who lied or distorted facts. Instead of reacting with anger, I started to ask: *What story are they trying to protect? What truth is too painful for them to face?* Understanding this softened my judgments and, in some cases, preserved relationships.

Years later, another film would strike me with equal force, though in a very different register. *12 Angry Men*, Sidney Lumet's courtroom drama, immersed me in the sweaty confinement of a New York jury room. I watched it in Spain in the late 1950s. The theater was grander this time, filled with cigarette smoke. On screen, twelve jurors argued, bullied, and bargained over the fate of a teenage boy accused of murdering his father.

The brilliance of the film wasn't just in Henry Fonda's quiet insistence on reason or Lee J. Cobb's thunderous rage. It was in how ordinary men let their hunger, boredom, and personal grudges weigh just as heavily as the evidence. One juror hurried to convict so he could catch a baseball game. Another projected his disappointment with his son onto the boy on trial.

I remember laughing afterward when I read that even real judges aren't immune to such weaknesses. One study showed that sentences were tougher before lunch and more forgiving afterward. Justice, it appears, relies not only on the law but also on whether the judge has eaten a sandwich.

Kurosawa's *Rashomon* and Lumet's *12 Angry Men* shaped my moral compass by showing me that every person distorts reality to maintain dignity and revealing how group decisions, even about life and death, often rely on prejudice, fatigue, and basic bodily needs.

Their lessons have stayed with me ever since. They taught me to be cautious of certainty, skeptical of group consensus, and attentive to the weaknesses hidden beneath reason's polished surface. Above all, they encouraged me to meet others not with blind trust or judgment but with a curious compassion for the stories they share – stories that, like mine, try to make sense of a world forever divided between truth and illusion.

The Detour

After making the decision to study medicine, I went to my dad, who was sitting alone in his comfortable chair, reading the paper, and smoking a cigarette. I was rolling his cigarettes with a small machine, when I brought it up, "Dad, I need to talk to you."

I used the strong, bulk tobacco he liked and the thinnest, high-quality papers I could find. I said, "After thinking about it, I've decided I want to study medicine."

My father looked up, surprised. He had a rare talent for showing presence without words: a quick nod, a glimmer in his eye, and suddenly I felt taller. He replied, "Good. The family needs a doctor. You'll help people. You'll make something of yourself."

Then Amelia entered. My stepmother didn't do glimmers. She was the boss of the family, and she didn't strategize. She crossed her arms, pressed her lips into a thin line, and replied, "Medicine? You? Impossible. Do you know how many years it takes? How much money do you have? You'll immerse yourself in books, and for what purpose? You're aware of the challenges young doctors face in finding employment. Many end up having to go to Africa to find work," speaking as if she were an expert on the subject.

I responded firmly. "But… I don't want to sell things. I'm not made for factory work. I don't want to be a business-man. I want something… something more meaningful."

"More meaningful?" said Amelia quickly. "What are you talking about? It's truly meaningful, my dear. What you need is to make real money. You think we're rich? Listen, pharmacy is the answer. You'll study in Madrid. Your father will buy a pharmacy when you graduate. I'll help at the count-er. It will be perfect. The company is secure, stable, profitable, and professional. It will work."

It seemed as if she had been doing her homework.

Agreeing softly, my father responded, "It's true. A pharmacy is not a disastrous idea."

And just like that, my grand medical dreams shrank to a mere prescription counter. I told myself that if I agreed to attend pharmacy school to please them, then I would be free to study what I truly wanted. The plan would be temporary. I could escape later, I thought.

So, I complied. The idea of living in Madrid, the big capital city of Spain, was exciting. Madrid felt like a different country compared to Valencia: bigger, faster, louder, freer, and more stylish. I moved into a student dormitory where a woman cooked meals for us. The house was filled with other friendly students, and the smell of fried foods was always lingering. At the Pharmacy School, my classmates were young, mostly women who were bright and talkative. To my surprise, I enjoyed some of the coursework. Geology fascinated me with its deep, intriguing timelines. Chemistry appealed to my logical side. But Botany truly enchanted me.

We took field trips into Madrid's forests, identifying plants and trees as if they were old friends. I kept a book with specimens of various plants, leaves, and ferns. I loved the precision of how leaves formed patterns and how branches split with almost mathematical obedience to hidden laws. I could sense that each plant was following a kind of code: two, then four, then eight leaves, or a spiral of growth hinting at its nutritional history, struggles, and bursts of abundance.

One night, chaos interrupted this academic rhythm: smoke, shouting, and the clang of firefighters' axes. The kitchen had caught fire. Students ran barefoot down the hallways. Pots clattered. Walls shook. And me? I slept through it. I opened my door the next morning, yawning, only to find half the kitchen missing. A whole wall was gone. Hmm, I thought. Must have been an eventful night. That was Madrid for me. Life was happening loudly, and I was still half-asleep, carrying out Amelia's plan like I was on an invisible leash.

Every day on my way to class, I passed the imposing facade of the medical school with its tall marble columns like a Greek temple and wide steps. Students in white coats were laughing, smoking, and moving with the effortless confidence of people whose futures seemed larger than mine. I slowed down each time, pretending to tie a shoe while watching them. That's where I belonged, I thought. I did not want to be counting pills nor standing behind a counter with Amelia.

By the time I went back to Valencia for the summer, I'd made my next decision.

*

One evening at the dinner table I said, "I'm sorry to tell you this, but I'm leaving the pharmacy school. I want to study medicine in Valencia instead." I paused to let the information sink in. "It'll be cheaper, and I can live at home."

Father replied calmly, "That makes sense."

Amelia rapidly followed between the sound of her slamming a pot, "Makes sense? What about the sacrifices we have made?"

"It's my life." I retorted with emphasis on "my life." I'm usually well controlled, but this time I lost it.

Amelia sensed she lost the argument and ran from the room. "You'll see, you'll regret it. Work for your money," she yelled.

That's when I learned that freedom always has a price. This was a price worth paying. I was punished with no allowance, but I could continue living at home. When you are financially dependent on your parents, you must navigate the situation carefully to avoid irritating them too much.

My brother quietly gave me some money on weekends so I could buy coffee and go to the movies. I also started earning my money by selling German mechanical calculating machines. These small, sleek devices with a handle were the best portable office calculating machines of their time in the last generation before electronic devices took over.

My father became my first customer, happy to replace his paper-pencil-calculated payroll with the rhythmic sound of gears. To my surprise, I realized I was proficient at sales. I paused for a moment. *What about becoming a businessman?* But immediately dismissed the idea.

Medical school brought its challenges, especially with Amelia trying to interfere with my exams. I would stay up late memorizing diagrams of anatomy and physiology, and Amelia would appear as a dark silhouette in my bedroom doorway, enforcing rules she had made up for the dorm. "Enough. Lights off. Go to bed. Now! You are not letting anybody sleep," she would say.

I turned off the light, pretended to go to bed, and waited quietly, listening for her footsteps to fade. After a while, I turned the lamp back on. Though this little game was silly, it strengthened my resolve. I learned that persistence, negotiation, sneakiness, and sometimes a detour is necessary to find the path you truly want.

Medical School in Valencia

I was caught between two hospitals in Valencia, the Old and the New, where the medical school sent us for our clinical training. Each place carried its rhythm, its ghosts, and its own lessons.

The Old General Hospital had been standing since 1512, when King Ferdinand the Catholic ordered the unification of the city's smaller hospitals into one. Walking through its stone arches felt like stepping back into centuries of medicine. The air smelled of antiseptic and age. Its echoing wards stretched long with patients' iron beds scattered and little thought for privacy. Medicine here was steeped in history, as though you could still hear the monks and physicians who had tended to the sick in centuries past.

Juan Luis Vives once wrote that hospitals were places where the sick were cured, orphans were raised, the blind were given refuge, and even the mad were clothed and sheltered. In

Valencia, that vision had been realized in this sprawling institution, though by the time I walked its corridors, it bore the scars of neglect.

Pedro, my best friend in medical school, and I made our rounds each afternoon, carrying far more responsibility than two half-trained students should. Medications were scarce and where newer drugs sometimes never even made it to the pharmacy shelves. We took to wandering the city, knocking on the doors of pharmaceutical representatives at their homes, collecting free samples to bring back to our patients. The nurses were nuns who lived inside the hospital, gliding through the wards in their white habits. Sometimes they'd vanish suddenly for prayer, leaving us to manage the patients alone.

The New Hospital, *El Clínico*, was a different story. The room was bright, clean, and spacious, but strangely empty. The rooms had more air but less life. No proper systems existed yet, so we had to act as doctors, nurses, and orderlies all at once. One evening, a group of us slipped out to a nearby cantina for supper, leaving the patients unattended. A visiting Swiss medical student chastised me for our carelessness, reminding me that in his country, they took turns so no patient was ever left alone. His words stung. For the first time, I realized how far behind Spain was in its standards of care. The problem wasn't laziness, it was poor management and an absence of structure.

Classes could be just as strange. I remember one pharmacology professor whose teaching method was to dictate lessons to a student at the blackboard while the rest of us dutifully copied them into our notebooks. It was as if knowledge itself were a ledger to be transcribed rather than not explored. Every subject had its own official textbook and that was all we were expected to know. Later, in the United States, I was astonished to find students swimming in sources from journals and endless shelves of books. Knowledge felt alive there — like it was moving.

In Valencia, my intellectual curiosity found a meaningful expression in the field of psychiatry. I joined a small group of students fascinated by psychoanalysis. Each week, we met with Dr. Pertejo, a local psychoanalyst, in a modest seminar room. At that time, psychiatry in Spain was largely practiced by neurologists who mocked us for pursuing dreams over science. To them, psychoanalysis was little more than fantasy compared to the rough edges of neurology. Still, we persisted. We divided the mind's suffering into two crude categories: neuroses and psychoses. It was straightforward, perhaps even naive, but it created opportunities.

Looking back, I realize that my education in Valencia wasn't only about medicine. It was about contrasts: between the medieval and the modern, the rigid and the improvisational, the local and the global. In the old wards of *El*

Clínico, heavy with history, I began to glimpse the wide, uneven world of medicine and the life I was about to step into.

Discovering the Dark Side of Psychiatry

My first real encounter with severely ill psychiatric patients happened when I was a medical student in Valencia, inside a dilapidated public asylum named after Padre Jofré. He was a compassionate friar who, back in 1409, did something extraordinary. The story goes that he once stopped a group of children from throwing stones at a madman in the street. Instead of calling for punishment, he preached compassion. From that point on, he fought to create a facility that would care for the mentally ill instead of discarding them. Out of that vision grew one of the earliest psychiatric institutions in Europe.

By the time I stepped through its heavy doors, the place was less a beacon of compassion and more a worn relic. The architecture still bore a faint grandeur, but behind it, a sense of confinement disguised as mercy lingered. The air smelled of disinfectant, cigarette smoke, and a sour odor that clung to the walls.

I attended staff meetings there, expecting serious discussions about patients and treatments, but what I experienced was disappointing. The psychiatrists (if you could call them that) never talked about the patients at all. They smoked nonstop, their fingers stained yellow, and the ashtrays filled faster than their notebooks. Tiny cups of espresso clattered on saucers as they argued politics, formed cliques, and circled each other in endless debates that had nothing to do with medicine. Not one of them stepped into the wards. The nuns, who crept through the halls, handled the genuine care of carrying trays, straightening sheets, and praying.

A story is lodged deep in my gut. A woman, who was severely disturbed, had been placed in solitary confinement. Days passed, maybe weeks and no one checked on her. By the time someone remembered her, she was dead.

Walking through those wards, I never saw "cases" or "diagnoses." I saw people with vacant eyes in search of something, with voices breaking into mutters or cries, with hands trembling as if memory itself had slipped through their fingers. They were not monsters. They were human beings who'd been wounded and cast aside but still carried a spark of dignity.

Even then, I could sense the delicate boundary between the healer and the patient, between sanity and madness, and between freedom and captivity. That line was far more porous than anyone in our clinical meetings dared acknowledge. In that place, discharges simply did not exist. Patients were admitted for life, as if their illness were a life sentence. The prevailing belief was simple and brutal: the seriously mentally ill could not be cured, could not improve, and must remain hidden from the world.

Later, when a representative from a European health organization visited our new medical school, a few of us students asked to speak with him privately. With him, I shared my observations of the neglect, the indifference, and the way individuals slipped through the gaps and disappeared. He listened without interrupting, his face revealing nothing. When I finished, he leaned back and said, almost gently, "This is not unique to Spain. The problem is systemic, deeply rooted. Change will not come from the top. If you want to make a difference, consider a career in psychiatry. Get the best training you can. Then come back and do better."

It wasn't the reassurance I was hoping for, but it was honest. And maybe that mattered more. A seed was planted that day, not of hope exactly, but one of resolve.

The Spanish Military and Me

In Franco's Spain, every young man was obligated to serve three years in the military. It was the invisible tax on youth, obedience paid in uniform. Every fiber of my being resisted the idea, but resistance was useless. My brother had served. I had seen him stiff in photographs, wearing an ill-fitting jacket that made him look less like a soldier than a schoolboy in costume. Somehow, he endured.

For me, there was an escape clause, though "escape" is perhaps too generous a word. University students could fulfill their duty through a program vaguely modeled after the American ROTC. It meant two summers of training, and at the end, a commission as an officer in the reserves. It was an offer you couldn't refuse. It was mandatory.

Ronda was my first stop, a town perched on the edge of a gorge, as if the earth itself had split open and decided to show off. We camped in tents, ten per site, surrounded by the usual smell of canvas, sweat, and boots. During the day we did drills and at night we enjoyed the comfort of camaraderie. On weekends, we headed into town where history seemed to press against us at every turn. Moorish staircases wound down into the gorge, worn smooth by enslaved Christians who carried water centuries ago. The Puente Nuevo arched above us like something sketched by a child with imagination. Even the swimming pool held a memory of the past, segregated by sex, with boys and girls forbidden to swim together.

It wasn't all deprivation. One summer break was spent with comrades on the beaches of Andalusia. The scent of salt, the girls in bright dresses, the nights stretching long with laughter felt like we had tricked the dictatorship itself into giving us a week of freedom.

At the end of the first summer, we became sergeants. By the end of the second summer, *alféreces* (junior officers). I even had a tailored uniform, complete with tall, polished leather boots. I looked like a poor man's General Patton, strutting through Andalusian dust. The third summer sent me north, to a base in Tarragona. Here, the absurdities of military life revealed themselves more clearly.

One evening, a few minutes before ten, I decided to test a rule in the manual: the canteen must close at 22:00 hours. My elders, the captains, lieutenants, even colonels, were still inside drinking as if Franco himself had decreed their right to bottomless glasses. I entered with a patrol of soldiers, announced with all the borrowed authority of youth that the canteen was closed, and ordered the bartender home. The silence that followed was thick. The officers that outranked me, despised me in that instant with their stares. Rules were rules, and I had caught them in their own net. One by one, like reluctant schoolboys, they shuffled off to their homes. I went to bed with the strange satisfaction of a mouse who had outwitted cats.

The next morning, the base buzzed. I overheard a captain marveling at the audacity of some *alférez* who had dared shut the place down. He assumed it was another officer, the one with a motorcycle and sunglasses who looked like he had ridden straight out of a Hollywood film. When I confessed it was me, he blinked in disbelief, and then, curiously, respect.

Perhaps it was that act of insolence, or maybe the article I later published in the Army Journal about what we now call PTSD, that earned me strange distinctions. I was chosen for the parade in Tarragona, boots gleaming as I marched down the avenues. And when Franco himself visited the city, I was placed on duty with the garrison. A pawn close enough to guard the king but never close enough to speak.

That was the way of Spain at the time. The gulf between the ranks was absolute. No captain or colonel ever approached me to offer a word, a correction, or even a nod. In the United States, I would later learn, hierarchy was strict but porous; you could at least imagine a conversation with your superiors. In Spain, the silence was the wall, and the wall was unbroken.

What did I learn? That power is not only in rank but in the refusal to be cowed. When you find yourself in a world of uniforms, whether that be military, academic, or professional, remember that your voice matters even when it trembles. Rules are not sacred because they are written. They are sacred only if they serve justice. And sometimes the actual parade in life is not the one where you march in step but the one where you quietly step aside, knowing you are already on your way to another, freer place.

Chapter 4:
Paris and London,
early 1960s

"The world is a book, and those who do not travel read only one page."

—Saint Augustine

Paris

"Paris," I murmured to myself as the taxi drove into the city from Orly Airport. "Paris!" The name itself was like a ray of light in my mouth.

From the window, boulevards sparkled in the late afternoon sun. The driver showed me a silhouette of a cathedral I knew from books: the dark towers of Notre Dame, like old guardians above the Seine.

But freedom came with an empty wallet. Parisian cafés gleamed with tiny tables and shining glasses, but the prices on their menus made me back away. Someone had told me where to find reasonably priced food: Mabillon, a university cafeteria near the Place de l'Odéon. You could purchase two meals a day for a single franc with a student card.

The next day, I found it. The line stretched out the door, a river of young faces. Inside, the place was enormous. Trays clattered, voices mingled in dozens of languages, and the smell of warm bread, soups, and something sweet wrapped around me. For the first time, I felt that the world might be kinder than I had imagined.

I carried my tray to a table and sat alone, watching the room with quiet wonder. Then, from across the hall, I saw someone familiar: Raul, a boy from Valencia I hadn't seen in years.

"Raul?" I called, half disbelieving.

He looked up, then broke into a grin and wove his way through the tables, tray balanced in his hands. "Vincent! What are you doing here?"

"What am I doing here? What are you doing here?" I laughed, and for a moment Paris felt smaller, almost intimate.

We sat together, talking quickly between bites. I remembered visiting his family as a boy and how their shelves lined with books had opened my world; Homer's *Odyssey, The Iliad*, and tales of gods and heroes had made me dream of lands beyond Spain's mountains. It felt like fate that we'd meet here, surrounded by the same kind of restless, curious souls we had once both only read about.

*

On the night before I left for London, I barely had enough francs left for the ferry ticket when my brother introduced me to a young British student. She was kind and beautiful in a casual, unselfconscious way and offered me a tiny room in her attic apartment for the night.

The building had no elevator. I lugged my suitcase up six flights, my shirt sticking to my back and breath short by the time we reached the top. The hallway smelled of dust, old wood, and boiled cabbage. Her room was barely bigger than a closet with one narrow bed, a small table, and a rug worn thin as paper.

She smiled, apologetic. "The toilets are down the hall," she said in careful French-accented English. "Best to use them early in the morning. Before they get busy."

I nodded, clutching my sleeping bag like a shield. She changed into a thin cotton gown, then slipped under the blanket. "We can share the bed," she offered matter-of-factly.

I froze.

Images flashed in my mind of an English woman on a beach in Valencia, years earlier, screaming at me for nothing more than saying hello. The memory hit like a slap: her sunglasses flashing, her voice slicing the quiet air, and my shame as I backed away.

What if this girl misunderstood? What if I rolled over in my sleep, touched her by accident, and embarrassed myself with a boner?

I forced a polite smile. "Thank you, but I have a sleeping bag," I said, unrolling it on the floor over the ragged rug.

She raised an eyebrow but said nothing. I climbed inside, fully dressed, and stared at the ceiling until exhaustion pulled me under.

Looking back, I laugh at my fear. At that time, I was just a boy on his first journey through the world: shy, overly cautious, amazed by everything, and not yet brave enough to seize these kinds of moments. I didn't know that casual sex existed. I believed that a woman would only invite a man to her bed after they had an ongoing relationship. I didn't want to leave a bad impression, but I may have left disappointment.

Crossing the English Channel

The day was bright, and a cool breeze slid over the deck, carrying with it the tang of salt and diesel. I stood there with my backpack hanging loosely over one shoulder, feeling both restless and thrilled. Ahead lay Great Britain. A place that, to me then, meant possibility, distance, and a step closer to a broader world I had only imagined.

The ferry was full. Children clung to their parents' hands, men smoked pipes that left a sweet, woody trail in the air, and women leaned against the railings with their scarves fluttering. I watched the tall, thin officers in crisp navy uniforms stride across the deck, sharply yet calmly, seeming so sure of themselves.

I was not certain. I wandered slowly, feeling the wooden boards vibrate beneath my feet, breathing deeply as the wind cooled the sweat on my back. Everything around me — the language, the faces, and the laughter — felt foreign.

That's when I saw her.

She stood in the center of the deck with a wooden stand before her and a sheet of paper pinned in place. She worked quickly. Her hand moved a heavy black pencil across the page, her eyes lifting every few seconds to scan the crowd and, I suspected, to scan me. Her gaze was focused but not unkind, as if she were capturing people rather than simply looking at them.

I lingered at a distance, pretending to admire the sea, but I was watching her. *Should I go over?* I thought. *What if she's annoyed? What if she laughs at me? What if I can't find the right words?* I tried recalling my English. I knew the verb *dibujar* — to draw. But what was the noun? *Dibujo*. It had to be something like a draw. My heart hammered in my chest. I told myself that if I didn't try, I would regret it forever. I stepped forward. When I reached her, she looked up and her blue-gray eyes met mine. She smiled.

I swallowed hard and said carefully, "Excuse me, young lady. Can I see your draws?"

Her smile faltered. She blinked, shocked, almost startled. For a beat, I panicked. *Did I say something rude or inappropriate?* I tried again, this time gesturing toward her drawings.

She stared at me for a second, then laughed softly, and the tension broke like a wave. She turned the paper toward me. The page was filled with quick, beautiful sketches: faces, silhouettes, and bits of the sea.

Only later, through a mix of words and gestures, she gently explained that "draws" meant something entirely different than "drawings."

Heat flooded my face, "Oh…I… sorry," I stammered.

But she smiled, as though my mistake had charmed rather than offended her. "It's okay," she said.

I walked away embarrassed but strangely proud. I had spoken. I had dared. And the world, instead of rejecting me, had answered with kindness.

Fog and a Smile: London

On my first visit to London, the city was performing exactly as advertised. A dreary, blustery rain swept down from the gray heavens, and a stubborn fog settled so thick I could barely see past my footsteps.

Feeling the chill in my bones and a kind of aimless melancholy that tends to accompany foreign streets, I ducked into the Underground. London's subway map was a complex network of intersecting colors and lines. I stared at the wall-sized map trying to figure out which direction to go, unsure where I was headed, just sure I needed to go somewhere. The subway map had a different logic than those in Madrid or Paris; more complex, it needed more decoding.

When the doors opened, I stepped into the train and found a place on a long wooden bench. At first, the car was crowded, packed with raincoats, overcoats, umbrellas, and unreadable British expressions. Slowly, people began to get off at their stops and the crowd thinned.

A young British woman sat on the bench directly across from me. She wasn't reading or distracted. She was looking straight at me. But not in the usual way people observe strangers as they pass. She was smiling.

It wasn't a polite or accidental smile. It was radiant and confident, like the expression of someone who had just uncovered a secret and didn't mind if you noticed. There was no awkwardness in her gaze. She gazed at me as if we were old friends. Her smile wasn't aggressive or flirtatious. It was soft, knowing, and almost amused. She acted as if she were the cat and I was the canary, already knowing how the story would end.

And I, well, I wasn't at my best that day. My English was shaky. I was worn out, foggy-headed, and uneasy with the labyrinth of tunnels that twisted beneath London's streets. I was worried I'd get lost. I felt far from home. So, I didn't say anything. I wouldn't have even known what to say.

The train continued to move, making stops inter-mittently. The moment held, then passed as she stepped off at her stop. We never spoke a word.

But she saw me, and I saw her.

In a city of millions, surrounded by strangers, she looked at me, as if saying, "You are not invisible."

And sometimes, that's all it takes to make you feel welcome.

Becoming a Man (the British Way)

I was twenty-four, a medical student in my senior year, still a virgin, and ready to experience what liberation from the moral fortress of puritanical Spain would be like. Losing my virginity was a big deal. A seismic shift. A before-and-after kind of moment.

In Spain, sex before marriage was like murder, talked about in hushed tones, possibly committed by godless foreigners but not something nice Catholic boys or proper *señoritas* did. Or so I believed. I had bought into the "Celibacy Until Marriage" narrative like it was gospel, even after I stopped being religious. It was the cultural soup I swam in.

Spanish girls also played their parts to perfection. So much so that if a hint of anything romantically erotic was mentioned their eyes would widen like you'd just suggested burning down the church. They clutched their chastity. I followed in accordance. I was a fool.

Looking back, I realize we were following a script. A cultural one that controlled our thoughts and actions as if we were marionettes.

The script of an era was already on its way out in most of Europe but still clinging to life in Franco's Spain. One-part medieval honor code, one part romanticized nonsense. A lot of talk about "female virtue" and "family name" and the terror of producing a bastard who'd be barred from inheritance and respectability. I swallowed it whole.

That summer in England, I was shadowing at a psychiatric hospital for a few weeks, something between an internship and a holiday. Room and board were free (a miracle), the system was socialized (another miracle), and tea and biscuits were served twice a day to patients and staff with the kind of ceremony usually reserved for royal christenings.

I'd never seen anything like it. Even the meals in the doctors' dining room were served by white-gloved waiters who lifted silver lids with a flourish, revealing boiled potatoes and steamed mystery meat with an elegance that somehow made it feel gourmet.

I was staying in a different building but ate my meals at the staff residence, which felt like a Hogwarts for grown-up mental health professionals. Among the staff living there were a few women I remember clearly. One was an older, bossy psychologist who scolded me for a missing button and told me I should learn to sew. She probably saw how hopeless I would be at that task, so she ended up sewing it for me anyway. There was a slightly odd, not-so-young psychiatrist, and a third lovely, younger psychologist with a quiet spark in her eye.

One night, something improbable happened.

Somehow, although I can't recall exactly how, I ended up in the young psychologist's bedroom. I indeed hadn't initiated it as I lacked the confidence, the language, and most importantly, the nerve. She looked at me and gently said, "Why don't you come into bed?"

She was already in a nightgown, and I could hardly breathe.

She introduced me to it. She showed me how it was done, like a teacher, and I was her student. It was miraculous. The experience was warm and surreal and ended almost before it began. For the first time in my life, I knew what it felt like to be in communion with another human being. It was beautiful, and I was thrilled and terrified at the same time. With all the sincerity I could muster, I kissed her, whispered, "thank you," and stealthily left her room.

I walked back to my place with the cold air on my face and a grin I couldn't wipe off. I had done it. I was a man. At last.

But then things got complicated.

The seasoned psychiatrist had caught wind, so she started inviting me to her apartment, dropping increasingly bold hints. I went along, more out of confusion than strategy, and to my surprise, I began to improve, technically speaking.

In love, the lover is the player, the body the instrument, and the moans the music. The women seemed appreciative. I felt like an inexperienced violinist who had just realized he could play a melody. My confidence bloomed.

One evening, as I approached the dining hall, I saw the two women, the psychologist and the psychiatrist, caught in a shouting match on the staircase. Yes, shouting. In public. In England. It was like watching the Queen throw a tantrum. I didn't understand a word, but I was pretty sure I was involved. I sneaked away without dinner, feeling both embarrassed and strangely proud. Women were fighting over me, a shy, awkward Spaniard!

Walking back to my quarters that night, I felt absurdly proud and deeply confused. *I was a man now, but what did that even mean?*

Nicholas, a tall, attractive medical student, approached me days later to confront me about my "behavior." He, too, had been seeing the young psychologist and was upset. I had unknowingly sparked a love triangle or quadrangle and shaken it up like a cocktail in a shaker. He spoke to me as if I were some incorrigible Casanova. I said nothing but thought, *if he only knew.*

I hadn't meant to cause a scandal. But there I was, right in the middle of one.

The psychiatrist, undeterred, invited me on a weekend trip to see some of Britain's landmarks. We boarded a bus, and I sat by the window. At the next stop, I looked out and there she was. The psychologist had just come out of a liquor store, clutching a brown paper bag with a bottle of whiskey peeking out. She looked miserable.

I wanted to jump off the bus, run to her, hold her, and say something to console her. The bus door hissed shut. My whole being screamed, I want to be with her. But I stayed on the bus like a dummy.

What complicated creatures we are. We flee from what we claim to want. We pursue what resists us. We bind our-selves to others with threads we do not fully see, then pull too hard or too late, leaving knots that bruise everyone involved.

Only later did I begin to understand how deceptive desire can be. We imagine fulfillment waiting just beyond the act itself, as if consummation were a door that, once opened, would finally quiet the hunger inside us. Instead, we often step through and find a strange emptiness waiting on the other side. Not failure. Not regret exactly. Just the realization that the promise was exaggerated. A trick of nature, perhaps, urging us forward without telling us the cost.

That summer, something shifted. I did not become a man in the theatrical sense — no conquest, no swagger, no sudden certainty. I became a man in a quieter way. I left with more awareness than I arrived with. Still flawed. Still uncertain. But less innocent about desire, and more attentive to the weight our choices place on ourselves and others.

It was the beginning — not of mastery, but of responsibility.

Chapter 5: Practicing Medicine in Spain

"As to diseases, make a habit of two things: to help, or at least to do no harm."

—Hippocrates

Spanish National Health Service, Valencia, 1962-3

Amelia, with an unnervingly clear view of the Spanish medical system, once warned me, "Unless you're ready to vanish into some mountain village or work for old doctors for peanuts, you'll starve. Even the old-timers can barely make a living in private practice, and to secure a job with the National Health Service, you need political connections to the Franco regime."

After finishing medical school in Spain, I was bursting with restless dreams, the kind that make you feel like your skin is too tight. Yet for all my ambition, I had nowhere to go. I had no job and no clear future. The only work available was patching holes in the National Health Service (El Sistema Nacional de Salud), as a temporary substitute, what they politely call *locum tenens* today. There was no reliable work available. The pay was pitiful, a fraction of a real doctor's salary, but I took every assignment that came my way.

The pace in those clinics was brutal. I was expected to see thirty or more patients in a single morning, and each one came armed with their own favorite cure. The nurses knew the routine better than I did; they had already filled out the prescriptions before I even arrived. It was my responsibility to sign them quickly and efficiently while maintaining the flow of the line. The patients didn't want medicine; they wanted reassurance and a little chemistry-fueled hope. Most asked for their usual placebos of vitamin injections and tonics to boost their *ánimo*, that wonderful Spanish word that straddles both "spirit" and "mood."

The truly ill were quickly sent to the hospital or would stay home to recover on their own. The entire operation was a grand act of collective self-deception. The nurses, the patients, the doctors equally played along. Medical services were provided for the convenience of the staff, and patients were satisfied with their placebos.

Some of my braver classmates took contracts in Africa. I heard stories of them in the Congo, where they vaccinated entire villages, faced diseases they had never heard of before, battled malaria, and performed surgeries they had only read about in textbooks. I admired them, but I had my plan. I wanted to learn a specialty, to grow, and find a place where medicine meant something more than political patronage and waiting your turn. I was looking for a place where perhaps I could do research and publish.

Rural Medicine, Vallada, 1963

When an offer came to help a rural doctor in Vallada, I jumped at it. Vallada is a quiet, sun-drenched hill town in the province of Valencia with a crumbling castle at its heights and narrow, cobbled streets. I played the role of *el médico del pueblo*, the country doctor, just like in the old films.

The doctor I worked for gave me a small room in his house. My mornings began with home visits with my black leather bag in hand, filled with the humble tools of my trade: stethoscope, thermometer, blood pressure cuff, otoscope, and ophthalmoscope. The afternoons were spent in the doctor's large living room, which doubled as a clinic. Outside, women in black shawls waited patiently, gossiping and fanning themselves while children played barefoot in the dust.

The people of Vallada were poor but proud. They had manners that no university could teach. Farmers with hands like bark treated me with reverence. "Doctor, my joints ache when I get up," one old man told me, gripping his cap like he was making a confession.

"Of course they do," I said. "You're eighty, and the earth has been fighting your body back."

He laughed, relieved that someone had at least noticed his years of hard work. Often, being seen and heard was enough. I learned that listening was sometimes more medicinal than anything in my black bag.

Patients brought me almonds, olive oil, and once, a live chicken, which I gave to the doctor's maid to cook for dinner. The town had no ambulances. When someone was gravely ill, a neighbor's truck or a relative's car became the emergency transport. The drive to the nearest hospital was long and winding, hours through mountain roads that seemed designed to test one's faith.

Despite the hardships, Vallada had its magic. The air smelled of rosemary and baked earth. The evenings belonged to laughter, guitars, and the glow of kerosene lamps. The more educated professionals did not align with the moral standards of the locals. I befriended the town's *curandera*, the local healer. She had once traveled to New York City and told me about a helicopter ride over Manhattan's skyscrapers, an image so absurdly modern against Vallada's medieval skyline that I laughed out loud in disbelief. She laughed too and told me,

"You're too restless for this town. You'll go far, Doctor." I couldn't help but wonder: *Would she be right?*

Psychiatry, Tarragona, 1963

After Vallada came Tarragona and with it, the other face of Spanish medicine. The psychiatric hospital was an old palace that had been converted into an asylum, another relic of an older age. Nuns patrolled the women's ward with keys jangling at their waists. Wealthy families paid handsomely to lock away inconvenient relatives like young daughters who couldn't say no. The poor were in large public wards with no privacy. The air reeked of urine and neglect, and the corridors echoed with murmurs, moans, and unanswered prayers. Spain's ghosts were alive and institutionalized.

Those experiences, some tender, others haunting, left me restless again. I wanted to see medicine practiced in a place where science wasn't strangled by bureaucracy and where obtaining a train ticket didn't require hours of waiting and an excess of patience.

Spain was my homeland, and I loved her — the warmth of her people, their generosity, their laughter that could outshine despair, but I never felt free there. Everyone else seemed happy, drinking wine, singing until dawn, savoring life as if nothing were missing. I envied them. *What prevented me from feeling as content as everyone else? Why did the same air that provided life to others suffocate me? Was I seeing things that others chose not to?*

Churches dripped with bad-taste rococo gold while their pews filled with silence. Professors dictated lectures word for word while students copied like obedient machines. Bureaucrats moved at glacial speed, guarding their little kingdoms of power and paper. Spain smiled, but her spirit was asleep.

Foreigners thought we were the happiest people on earth. And maybe we were, but I wasn't. I longed for something else.

My escape began in a theater, of all places. As a medical student, I led a drama group and staged plays by modern European writers whose voices carried the pulse of freedom. I participated in a classic Greek play at the Roman Theater in Sagunto. Once, I posted a flyer with a quote from Ortega y Gasset. The next day, the student union summoned me, reprimanded me, and shut us down. The words of Spain's greatest philosopher had been deemed subversive. That day, I understood censorship not as an idea, but as a living, choking thing.

Years later, when I began reading the works of British and American historians, I realized how much of Spain's past had been rewritten or erased. We were a country proud of our heritage and history. But in-depth knowledge and discussions were lacking.

I applied for a job in the United States, but the Green Visa was a slow miracle that could take years. Spain was not on the favorite list of countries for immigration.

Suddenly, a lifeline appeared. A friend who had moved to Switzerland called.

"I need someone to cover my job for a month in Payerne," he said. The hospital is a small surgical hospital. You'll like it."

"But I'm not a surgeon," I protested.

He laughed. "Doesn't matter. I'll show you what to do. Just come."

That was all I needed. I packed my bags in a rush with a feeling I can still sense in my chest. Boarding the train, I felt like a prisoner fleeing captivity. I didn't know what I would find on the other side, only that I was headed toward a different Europe, one that had lived in peace for centuries while the rest of the continent tore itself apart.

Part II.
EUROPE

*"Europe is made by its cities. Each one is
a chapter in humanity's story."*

—Goethe

Chapter 6: Switzerland and England

> *"In Switzerland it is impossible to be unhappy. The mountains will not allow it."*
>
> —John Steinbeck

> *"England is an everlasting mood: cloudy, introspective, and quietly resistant to change."*
>
> —Virginia Wolf

Payerne, 1963

I arrived in Payerne late at night. The friend who had called me quickly welcomed me and left at dawn. He was expected to work the next morning in the hospital's surgical suite at six o'clock. I was in scrubs, practicing how to clean my hands and nails properly, pretending I knew what I was doing.

No one handed me a scalpel. Luckily, most of my work involved preparing pre-op charts, following up on post-op patients, and translating between French and Spanish-speaking patients and staff. To my surprise, I found that I was useful, and the staff liked my work.

The hospital was quiet, clean, and humane, which meant it provided a comfortable environment for patients. People were kind and patients were respected and respectful. Even the hospital food was excellent. Everything ran smoothly, like a Swiss clock.

After a few weeks, the medical director called me into his office and said, "Would you consider staying here permanently? We could arrange a position."

It was tempting. Very tempting. But I said no.

I told him I'd already made plans to spend time at the Hôpital de Cery in Lausanne, a renowned psychiatric center. I wanted to learn more. I wanted to grow, to thrive, to study the mysteries of human behavior in the best places I could find.

The world had cracked open, just enough to let the light in. And I wasn't going to let that go.

Lausanne and Hôpital de Cery, 1963

I arrived in Lausanne with the urgency of someone who believed the world itself might vanish if he didn't seize it quickly. The city stretched out like a watercolor: pale buildings climbing steep streets, the blue shimmer of Lake Geneva below, and beyond it, the Alps rising like a promise I didn't fully understand yet.

My friends from Valencia had spoken of Hôpital de Cery in reverent tones, as if it were more a sanctuary than a hospital. "You must see it," one said. "The hospital is immaculate, clean, and modern. They treat the patients with tremendous respect and consideration. You can learn a lot there."

And they were right.

Set among vineyards and gentle green hills, Cery felt alive, as if the buildings themselves had absorbed the decades of theories and dreams that had come to fruition inside the walls.

I had no official position as they had none to offer, but the hospital's director allowed me to stay. In exchange for room and board, I could attend staff meetings, lectures, and case discussions. For a young man hungry for knowledge, it was like stepping through a secret door into a world that had been waiting for me.

Cery was not just a place you visited; it was a place that watched you in return. Its long hallways faintly smelled of polish and old paper. The nurses' shoes tapped steadily across the floors. Through wide windows, I often saw patients wandering the lawns, their coats buttoned up even in warm weather, their eyes elsewhere, some murmuring to invisible friends, others staring at the mountains as if trying to return to a lost life. Some chronic schizophrenic patients had lived there for decades, and their records contained several thick volumes. I thought it would be a beneficial schizophrenia study to follow the course of those patients. I started to collect data from some of them, hoping that someday I would return and see how their illness had progressed. Before I left, I sent the data I had collected to the hospital director just in case he wanted to follow up.

I remember asking one of the senior doctors, "Do they ever go home?"

He shrugged lightly. "For many, this is home. The mind can build a world so complete it no longer asks to leave."

But it wasn't just the patients who captivated me. Doctors came to Cery from all over the world who were brilliant, strange, and endlessly curious. Around coffee tables, they argued in quick, accented French: Freud vs. Jung, dreams vs. neurotransmitters, the old psychoanalytic guard resisting the new voice of biology. I sat quietly at first, notebook open, but when I dared to speak, I measured each word like a coin I couldn't afford to waste.

Some afternoons, a few of us would take the train to Geneva for lectures. I still remember one. The hall was packed, and the air charged. Jean Piaget himself stood at the podium with his gray hair brushed back and voice firm yet almost playful as he talked about the evolution of human thought.

"Only education," he said, pausing as if to let it sink in, "is capable of saving our societies from collapse, whether sudden or slow."

I quickly jotted down the words and underlined them twice. Something in those words felt aimed directly at me. He discussed assimilation and accommodation and how knowledge isn't just added but reshapes the learner. I realized that this was my life. I could see that each new country, each new language, each hospital and new patients were pushing me to adapt, grow, and rebuild myself little by little.

*

It wasn't all theory and books, Switzerland offered another kind of education, too.

Her name was Angeline. She was a kind medical student with calm eyes, precise French, and a curiosity that matched my own. We met after a lecture and within days, we were walking together beneath trees heavy with late-summer leaves.

"You're not Swiss," she said one evening, laughing softly as I tried to pronounce *Röstigraben*.

"No," I admitted. "But maybe I could be."

She tilted her head, studying me. "You like it here that much?"

I looked out toward the lake, its surface silver in the fading light. "It's clean. Ordered. Beautiful. Even the mountains look as if they've agreed to stand still."

Angeline smiled, "Then stay."

And I nearly did. With her, I saw a Switzerland beyond Cery's walls: the jagged glory of the Matterhorn at dawn, the quiet perfection of Lake Lucerne, the valleys of Interlaken, and the dizzying cable cars that carried us to ski resorts. In Geneva, she showed me through history, explaining Switzerland's stubborn neutrality with pride.

"Here," she told me once, standing on a bridge over the Rhône, "we learned to survive by avoiding wars we didn't need to fight."

Weekends blurred into a collage of train tickets, mountain air, and her voice naming peaks I still remember. I started to imagine a life there: speaking French fluently, working at Cery, building something permanent.

But then came the letter from England with a position, a salary, and a chance to strengthen my English — the language I would need for the next step, the one that would carry me across the ocean.

The night before I left, Angeline and I stood on a hillside above Lausanne. Below us, the city glowed softly.

"Do you have to go?" she asked.

I hesitated, then nodded. "Yes. England first. Then, America."

"Will you come back?"

I wanted to say yes. Instead, I said what I believed, "Part of me will stay here."

And it has. Even now, I can close my eyes and see those mountains and feel the quiet dignity of that country and the people I met there. Cery taught me that the mind is as vast and layered as the Alps themselves and that once you have looked out from such a height, some part of you never comes down.

Littlemore Hospital Near Oxford, 1964-1965

The English winter carried a dampness that seemed to seep into my bones. Each morning, as I walked across the grounds of Littlemore Psychiatric Hospital, the grass glittered with frost, and the red-brick buildings exhaled a chill. I had come here, half by choice and half by necessity, while waiting in Madrid for a U.S. visa that refused to arrive. My plan was simple: work, learn English, and keep moving toward the larger life I imagined in America.

The National Health Service hired me as a senior house officer, "a resident," in their terms. I was proud of that title. Dr. Duffield, my consulting psychiatrist, had written me a letter of recommendation, a kindness I hadn't expected. I felt almost exhilarated. There was a small house for staff near the hospital grounds where I could live, and I had patients to care for, new colleagues to meet, and a language to master.

But beneath the surface, Littlemore was not as warm as its name suggested.

The nurses — some kind, some guarded — watched me with a mix of curiosity and skepticism. I could feel it in the silence after I entered a ward, in the way conversations paused just a beat too long. Later, I would understand why. There were invisible hierarchies here — old resentments and prejudices that clung like the damp air: against the Irish, against Southern Europeans, against anyone whose skin carried a darker shade.

I didn't quite fit their categories. My hair was blond; my eyes were blue. "Where are you from?" a nurse once asked, squinting as though my answer might change something.

"Spain," I said.

She raised an eyebrow. "You don't look it."

*

One morning, while making rounds, I saw an elderly patient, a frail man with dementia, sitting in a corner, one eye darkened to a deep purple. I knelt beside him.

"What happened?" I asked softly. He mumbled something I couldn't catch.

A nurse explained briskly, "He was agitated last night. Tried to hit one of the staff."

"And so?" I looked at her.

"He was restrained," she said, her tone flat.

I studied the man's trembling hands. "He wasn't just restrained," I said. "Someone hit him."

The room shifted. Chairs stopped moving. Other nurses glanced at each other but said nothing. I felt a warmth rising in my chest, not anger exactly but something close to it.

"This is not acceptable," I said. "There are other ways to manage agitation. He could have been calmed, guided, held, not struck."

Later, one of them pulled me aside. "Doctor, you could report this to the NHS. But understand what that means. The nurse responsible could lose his job. And your life is here," she shrugged, "it will get harder."

That night I sat in my small room, staring at the frost forming on the windowpane. I thought about the old man's blackened eye, about the nurse's warning, and about the children I had treated in Switzerland. These were fragile bodies whose vulnerability demanded gentleness, not force. In the end, I didn't file an official report to the NHS. Instead, I gathered the staff and turned it into a teaching session about how to de-escalate agitation without violence. Dr. Duffield agreed with my choice. I knew the nurses would never fully trust me after that.

*

When December came, the hospital halls brightened with tinsel and paper garlands. I watched from the edges as staff prepared for the Christmas party with laughter in the break room and trays of mince pies carried past. A large ward had been cleared and adorned with lights, and trays of food and drink. There was a rare sense of excitement among the staff members, and I heard murmurs that they had sent out invitations for the evening festivities. I hadn't received one, but I assumed attending would be fine. I worked there after all.

That assumption turned out to be a mistake.

As I arrived and began chatting with a nurse, a hospital administrator approached me. "Do you have an invitation?" he asked. I admitted I didn't. "This event is by invitation only," he said bluntly, then walked away.

It stung but it didn't surprise me after seeing what had happened in the ward. Beneath the surface of polite English manners, I had already sensed the subtle yet persistent condescension aimed at foreigners, especially those of us from Southern Europe. To many, dark-haired, olive-skinned men from Spain, Italy, or Greece didn't quite meet the Anglo-Saxon ideal. The prejudice was quiet, coded, and rarely acknow-ledged aloud, but it was there.

As I stepped out into the cold that Christmas night, I realized something more profound than personal rejection. I was shown that in some places, your labor is welcome, but not you as a person.

*

The town of Oxford itself was kinder. I discovered evening classes at the university where rooms filled with adult learners like me, all trying to stretch themselves beyond their daily lives. Twice a week I sat in a wooden chair, my notebook open, discussing George Orwell's *Animal Farm.*

The words stirred something in me. "All animals are equal, but some animals are more equal than others." It felt uncomfortably familiar to these hierarchies, this quiet cruelty disguised as order. Orwell had fought in my homeland during the Spanish Civil War. He had seen, as I was beginning to see, how noble ideals could twist into something darker when ideology, fear, and power entered the room.

My goal was still to go to America, to immigrate there. I hoped that the country founded on the utopian ideals of the Enlightenment would be different from old Europe.

My Psychedelic Experiences

In the early 1960s, psychedelics were suddenly everywhere. People spoke about them with excitement as if they were keys to a new level of understanding. The idea was seductive and straightforward: take a pill, alter your state of consciousness, and discover truths about yourself that everyday life keeps hidden. At the time it seemed like psychedelics were the new frontier to be explored.

I was a young medical student then, fearless, curious, and naïve. A Sandoz representative came to the hospital and handed out tablets of psilocybin and LSD to medical students and young doctors. At the time, the company believed these substances had promise. They wanted physicians to try them firsthand.

I arranged my first psychedelic session at Padre Jofre Psychiatric Hospital in Valencia. A psychiatrist agreed to monitor me and record an EEG. The whole thing was filmed. I still have the video. The setting was cold and clinical — not exactly the ideal environment for a mind-altering experience.

What I remember is this: my hearing became sharp, almost too sharp. I could hear two clinicians talking about me in the hallway and their voices felt uncomfortably close. I felt a mild paranoia, not overwhelming, but enough to remind me that the mind can turn against itself when pushed.

When the session ended, the psychiatrist told me I had "excellent mental health" because I had not hallucinated or acted strangely. I was still under the influence though and I knew enough not to go home. I walked the streets of Valencia for hours until I felt steady again.

Years later, when I worked at Littlemore Hospital near Oxford, I tried a psychedelic again, LSD. This time it was with a British psychologist. We agreed to take it together under the supervision of a friend, an Argentine psychiatrist. He handed each of us a tablet of Thorazine to end the experience if it became too much.

The experiment did not teach me anything profound about the universe, but it did complicate my personal life. I developed a foolish attachment to the psychologist. She did not feel the same way. My affection turned into resentment, then slowly faded. It was a small, private lesson in human behavior, nothing mystical about it.

As for my "mission to save the world," psychedelics cured me of that, too. After a few experiences, I realized the world did not need saving. Many people, far more capable than I, were already working to make it better. My role was simpler: help where I could and know my limits.

Psychedelics are back in fashion. The main substances being studied today include: Psilocybin from certain mushrooms which can loosen rigid thought patterns and open the heart, LSD which alters perception and thinking for many hours and can overwhelm some individuals, MDMA which reduces fear and helps trauma survivors revisit painful memories safely, and Ketamine which acts quickly for depression by producing a brief shift in awareness and boosting neuroplasticity.

Each has potential benefits. Each carries risks.

What do I think of them now? Based on my experience and knowledge of how they impact the brain: First, never use them alone. These are not party drugs. They are powerful substances that work deeply on the mind. The experience can change wildly depending on your mood, your environment, and the people around you. Second, they can be helpful for some people, but only with a trained therapist and only with preparation. Please know what you hope to learn or resolve. And finally, you need someone to guide you through the experience and help you make sense of it afterward.

Psychedelic therapy is not magic. It isn't a menace either. It's a tool, one that can help some people break old patterns or see their life from a new perspective. But it cannot replace the slow, steady process of healing. A psychedelic may open a door. Walking through it remains the traveler's task.

Lavigny, 1965

In the summer of 1965, I found myself in motion but not yet in flight. I left my position as Senior House Officer at Littlemore Hospital, certain that I had already received my U.S. visa. I imagined myself boarding a ship or plane, finally crossing the Atlantic. But in Madrid, reality caught up; Spain wasn't on America's priority list. While British, French, and German doctors were welcomed swiftly, Spaniards, like me, had to wait.

I found myself with idle time, a sensation I detested. Restlessness drove me back to Switzerland, to a place that felt both safe and foreign, where I could work until the paperwork decided my fate.

Lavigny, a village tucked among rolling vineyards and quiet fields, where a stone hospital overlooked the lake and mountains wasn't just a hospital, it was a refuge for children whose bodies betrayed them daily. They were small — many of them far too small for their ages — and their limbs sometimes twisted by birth or seizures. Some stared with eyes that seemed to ask questions they could not speak. Others let out a sudden, sharp, unfiltered laugh that called through the corridors like an unexpected bell ringing.

The official name was *Centre Neurologique et Éducatif de Lavigny*, but we all simply called it "the Institution." The director, Dr. Michel Tchicaloff, carried himself with patience which he used in both emergencies and endurance. My two colleagues, Dr. Henkins from Italy, and Dr. Rallo, a fellow Spaniard, were warm, practical men. In the humid July evenings, we compared notes, watched EEG tracings like detectives staring at a crime scene, and wrote what would become my first published paper: evidence that intravenous diazepam could halt *status epilepticus*, the most terrifying seizure storm a child's brain could suffer.

I remember one boy with thin wrists and eyelashes too long for such a pale face would experience seizures that were violent and unrelenting, until the injection slid into his vein. On the EEG screen, chaos would suddenly fall quiet, the wild spikes flattening into something that resembled peace. In those moments, I imagined his mind like a lake without wind.

Outside the wards, Lavigny felt deceptively calm. Nurses moved softly, speaking French in voices that reminded me of lullabies. One of the nurses, a smiling woman with red hair tucked under her cap, handed me her motorized bicycle one evening.

"Pour vous détendre un peu," she said, "to relax."

I wanted to escape the hospital walls, to outrun the anxious thoughts of visas and unknown futures. The bike was small, harmless looking. I started down the narrow road lined with vines and golden light.

The next village sat higher than I expected. Going up was almost pleasant with the slow hum of the motor, the smell of cut grass, and the warm air on my face. But coming down was another story. At first, it was thrilling with the rush of wind and the vineyards blurring into green streaks. Then the speed grew wilder. My hands tightened. I hovered over the brakes, terrified to grip too hard. If I braked suddenly, I'd fly. I leaned forward, trying to stay balanced, heart hammering as the bike roared faster than I thought it could.

For those endless seconds, I could see everything, and I thought, *not like this. I cannot die on a borrowed bike on a Swiss hill before I even reach America.*

Somehow, I reached the bottom intact. My legs were trembling when I parked the bike back where I found it. I said nothing about the incident. Pride, fear, or maybe shame kept me silent.

At night, in my small white room, I began to dream. I dreamt of ships sailing away without me. I saw vast oceans and the Statue of Liberty shrouded in fog. Sometimes I woke up feeling tight in my chest and with clenched fists, as if I had been holding onto something too tightly to let go. They were something like anxiety attacks, my unconscious mind worrying about an uncertain future.

When the summer ended, I left Lavigny with gratitude and a quantum of sadness. My Swiss girlfriend, Angeline, met me in Madrid. We walked together through dry August streets while she tried to reassure me — about the visa, about America, and about us. But beneath her tenderness was another truth. As we held hands, we were already parting again.

Preparing to Cross the Ocean

The kindness and competence I experienced in Europe steadied me. The fact I was welcomed in Europe made me feel whole. It was the first time I felt I might belong somewhere. I had left my country carrying a burden. Spain under Franco was poor, shuttered, and provincial, but I missed it. I arrived in Paris, London, and Switzerland with the suspicion that everyone would sense my smallness, that my accent and my provincial habits would betray me. I braced myself for rejection, the quiet disdain of strangers. And while there were moments when xenophobia drifted in the air, I never felt its sharpest sting. What I found surprised me: doors opened, hands were extended, and laughter was shared.

Still, the differences astonished me. From the windows of trains, Swiss villages looked like abandoned film sets. Streets stood empty with no children running, no elders leaning on canes, no women gossiping under the sun. In Spain, life spilled into the plazas, voices rising, chairs dragged outside, neighbors quarreling over politics or football. In Switzerland, silence pressed. It was unsettling, as if I were staring at a stage from which all the actors had fled, hidden behind a discipline of privacy I could not fathom.

Even the toilets told their story, immaculate, gleaming, each stall a small temple. But the entry cost a franc. I recall thinking, "The wealth of a nation is evident in its bathrooms." The rich keep them spotless; the poor are reminded, even in a most human need, that they do not belong.

And then there was restraint, the deliberate muffling of emotion. In Lausanne, friends would hush me with a finger to their lips: "Not so loud. People will stare."

But as Spaniards, how could we help it? Our voices rose like trumpets at a dinner table, in a train station, or anywhere we gathered. Arms flailed; faces shone with feeling. In Zurich, I watched locals smile, almost bemused, at families from the French cantons embracing and shouting their farewells on train platforms. To those observers, the sight of Latins openly displaying their affections in public was comedic. To me, it was simply life.

Paris taught me other lessons. The cabdrivers, with their unmatched rudeness, outdid New York. In England, hospital staff meetings adopted a different rhythm that was measured, polished, and with emotions kept in check. Speech became a performance, careful and dignified, with a superior tone. I remember wondering if I should learn to wear that same mask of control, to trade my warmth for their poise.

Beneath customs and surface gestures, I found something real; people are tender everywhere. Loneliness creeps into every language. Desire, too. Laughter, longing, and the need to be seen — none of it changes when you cross a border.

I was proud of how I traveled through Europe. My medical degree became a passport. With it, I could work anywhere, find shelter, and make a living. I learned that the world could be mine to explore. These were not small revelations to a young man bearing the weight of self-exile.

The memory contains more than just the thrill of discovery. It encompasses the pain of separation, the understanding of the fragility of belonging, and the significant reliance on the generosity of others. What I once saw as adventure, I now understand as initiation, the start of learning how to live in exile, with love, caution, and always with hope.

*

Not long ago, a Spaniard friend asked me, "Why did you want to move to the United States?"

On the surface, it seems like an easy question to answer, but memory is never simple. It carries a constellation of moments, each flickering like stars along a road I once walked.

If I reach back, the trail begins in the dim cinemas of postwar Spain. The projector rattled and America unfolded in wide horizons. Westerns gripped me most. I watched men who lived by their code, quiet until injustice arrived at their door, then steady, unflinching, and quick to act. They weren't lords or heirs; their strength lay in choice and moral courage. To a boy growing up under Franco, where status was inherited and the future was limited, that kind of freedom seemed like a form of salvation.

In these films, the women were strikingly different. They were lively, spirited, bold, and less constrained by the chains of propriety that kept Spanish women silent. On those screens, I saw not just romance but the possibility of a life where love could be freer and less burdened by tradition.

As a medical student in Valencia, I discovered another America, one that was hidden between the pages of *JAMA*, the *Journal of the American Medical Association*. I read about psychiatry training programs that paid their students. In Spain, you paid to be trained. There, you worked and starved until the privilege of experience was finally yours. But in America, they promised to teach and pay you at the same time. It felt revolutionary.

Of course, I was not only running toward something; I was also fleeing. Home had become unbearable. My stepmother's shadow darkened every room, and I felt my spirit shrinking within the confines of that house. America became a lifeline, not just a dream. To leave was to breathe again.

When word spread that I had received the visa, everything changed. My family and friends regarded me as though I had won a divine lottery. Their voices softened, and their hands lingered on my shoulder. It wasn't just permission to travel I had been granted; it was permission to imagine a different life.

I remember the day I walked past the U.S. Marines outside the American Embassy in Madrid. They stood like the men from those Westerns of my childhood, tall, impassive, and their uniforms immaculate. Inside, the paperwork was endless. The same question circled back again and again: *Had I ever belonged to the Communist Party?* No. However, in those Cold War days, to appease McCarthy, everyone should be a suspect, and the virus of socialist ideas should be kept away from the U.S. shores in the same way that foreign species of plants or animals should be quarantined to prevent new diseases coming into the New World.

Angeline was with me then. In the evenings before my departure, she trained me in mock dialogues, teaching me how to say no to American women. We laughed until our ribs hurt.

Her jealousy was wrapped in play, though a sadness lingered. She knew the ocean would widen into something neither of us could cross. Love, too, was something I would be leaving behind.

America waited. The University of Vermont had accepted me into its psychiatry program. I was to rotate through hospitals, learn from patients, and begin again.

When I look back now, I see more than ambition. I know the boy in the cinema, his face lit by the glow of Westerns, yearning for a different life. I see the young man suffocating at home, clutching a visa like a key. I see Angeline laughing through her tears.

Why did I want to move to the United States? The most accurate answer is this: America was not just a place on a map. For me, it was a door, a promise to a freer life, where someone without money could thrive, and I was desperate to step through that gate.

Part III: AMERICA

"The welfare of America is intimately linked with the welfare of all humanity."

—Lafayette

Chapter 7: Coming to America

"America is not a country; it is an idea."

—Bono

Crossing the Ocean

September 25, 1965. After years of waiting and dreaming, I boarded a plane from Madrid to New York.

My destination: Burlington, Vermont.

My purpose: freedom and a new life.

In the Spanish public health system, I had become little more than a vitamin dispenser. One afternoon, I saw dozens of patients. Just prescriptions in and patients out, with no time for a meaningful conversation. Resistance was futile.

But America — ah, America! I had admired the country from afar: its boldness, its creativity, and even its contradictions. America. The word shimmered with possibility. I had come so far already and was now a trained doctor, eager to specialize, to dive into the mind's mysteries, and to maybe even make discoveries that mattered.

The thrill was intertwined with a sense of unease. *What would this new land be like? Would I be welcomed, folded gently into the great, chaotic fabric of American life? Or would I find myself on the outside looking in, a stranger in a place that demanded more than just skill, but belonging, too?*

I thought about the accent I carried and the slight awkwardness I felt when speaking English. Would they see me for who I was — a soul yearning to contribute — or only as a foreigner, another outsider, with strange vowels and strange ways?

Kennedy Airport would be my first test. From there, another flight northward, to Burlington, Vermont, a small city that was cold and unfamiliar, nestled in a state I had only glimpsed on maps. Vermont sounded quiet, distant from the roaring myths of New York and Los Angeles. Perhaps it would be a place of refuge.

Beneath the anxiety, a strong current of hope still ran. I carried within me the momentum of generations: the dreams of my parents, the sacrifices of those who had come before, the private, stubborn belief that life could be larger than the one I had left behind.

*

America was not a promise given freely. It was a challenge I was willing to meet.

In the quiet roar of the plane, a strange certainty rose inside me. Whatever awaited on the other side of the ocean — acceptance, rejection, triumph, or struggle — it would become part of my story.

In my mixed emotion, I longed for connection. There was a young Spaniard nearby about my age. His clothes were finer, and his manner polished with the easy confidence of someone born into privilege. Yet something about him felt closed, distant, and he carried a subtle air of self-importance that made him seem unreachable. There was no invitation in his glances, only the polished armor of condescension.

I turned elsewhere and found a warmer path. A middle-aged American woman sat a few rows away with an open face and easy smile. I gathered my courage and asked if I could sit beside her. She welcomed me without hesitation, as if we had known each other in some forgotten life.

Grateful, I leaned into the space she offered and asked her about America, about what I might expect and what I should know.

For the first time since boarding the plane, I felt an authentic glimpse of what I hoped America could be — a place where, if you reached out with an open heart, someone might reach back.

As we spoke, she leaned in a little closer, her voice low as if offering a secret meant only for those just beginning their journey.

"America," she said, "is a country of extremes. You'll find the very best of people, doctors, scientists, dreamers who change the world. But you'll also find the worst, the Mafia, organized crime, and corruption lurking in the shadows. It's a land of light and darkness, often side by side."

I listened, absorbing every word as if they were directions on a map.

"Americans care about skills," she continued. "They respect what you can do. It doesn't matter where you come from or what your name sounds like. If you have something to offer, the doors will open for you. Maybe not right away, but they will."

Her words settled deep inside me, planting themselves like seeds in new soil. I would carry them with me into the bright unknown — a quiet compass for the life I was about to begin.

When we landed at Kennedy Airport, I boarded a smaller plane that finally touched down at the modest Burlington airport late that evening. The informality of American life immediately struck me. The atmosphere was casual, almost carefree.

Women stood waiting with rollers still in their hair, chatting easily, as if they were picking up groceries rather than greeting arrivals from distant places. In Spain, this would be like arriving at the opera in your underwear.

Outside, I stared in awe at the long, gleaming cars lined up at the curb. Limousines are what they called them, carrying only one or two people. I had never seen anything like them before. In Spain, such extravagance would have been reserved for royalty, not everyday life. *This is luxury,* I thought, *this is an example of unnecessary, extravagant, wasteful wealth — American style.*

A driver met me, and soon I arrived at the hospital residence where my new life would begin. A simple but sufficient room had been prepared for me. That night, I could hardly sleep. My mind raced ahead, imagining what the coming days would hold at the hospital, at the University of Vermont, and in the vast, unknown country that had now become my home.

Lying there in the dark, with only the hum of distant traffic outside my window, a melody floated into my mind like a voice from another lifetime, "Que será, será, whatever will be, will be. The future's not ours to see…" Doris Day replayed in my head, singing that song from the Hitchcock movie I had seen in Spain in 1956, *The Man Who Knew Too Much.*

I hummed the tune, allowing its simple wisdom to embrace me like a blanket. It was true. I could not predict what awaited me in this new land. I could only step forward, day by day, heart open, ready to meet whatever came.

I finally closed my eyes and surrendered to sleep, cradled by the quiet hope that somehow, some way, everything would find its place. Somewhere beyond the darkness, a new life was already waiting for me, as inevitable as the dawn.

First Impressions

My first morning in America, I walked into the hospital lobby and found a police officer waiting by the reception desk. His uniform was pressed and he carried a revolver at his hip. He nodded politely as if nothing were unusual. To me, it was astonishing. In Spain, only the *Guardia Civil* carried weapons, and they drew their guns only when danger was real. Here, danger seemed pre–approved. I thought: *Have I entered the Wild West?*

Men were bigger — almost inflated. Their biceps looked engineered, as if a secret ingredient had been added to their breakfast. Steak and potatoes, I guessed, protein for patriots. For my generation in Spain who grew up during the Civil War and post-war years, meat was rare, and growth not assured. Here, size felt like a social expectation. You needed a gym membership just to keep up.

Women were different too — direct, conversational, and curious. Many were boldly brave in ways I wasn't used to. They spoke their minds. They made choices without permission. They carried a toughness that hinted at loneliness. Without the shield of close family, I sensed they lived more exposed, more at risk.

In Spain, family members all stood behind us like walls. In America, people seemed to stand alone.

I noticed the machines next. America hummed with machinery like a second heartbeat. Highways stretched to the horizon — six lanes wide like runways for a new century. Trucks, enormous trucks, ruled the road. They looked like dinosaurs on wheels, hauling across the continent night and day.

In Vermont, the moment snow touched the ground, snowplows emerged like soldiers — cleaning, pushing, conquering. The machines never slept. In Spain, we would wait for the sun. Here, time was an enemy and the enemy had to be fought by machine.

Then there were guns. Guns in sporting stores, in catalogues, at outdoor fairs. In Vermont, hunting season felt like a regional holiday. On Sunday evenings, I saw deer carcasses hanging from car hoods. I also caught deer frozen in headlights, dazed, blinking, crossing the road, stepping into darkness with a limp. It bothered me to watch living creatures treated like moving targets. A resident from Argentina proudly bought a rifle "powerful enough to kill an elephant." He showed me the bullets, thick as my thumb. It disgusted me. I had learned to shoot in the Spanish military, but taking a life for entertainment felt like a betrayal of everything I believed medicine stood for.

Years later, the guns became ubiquitous, grew more numerous, and the headlines heavier. Children were being shot and dying in classrooms. Office workers were also dying of bullets at work, even in coffee shops, churches, and movie theaters. And politicians stood still. "Second Amendment," people said, as if guns had ancestors worth defending. I wondered: *Do they genuinely believe freedom depends on firepower, or have they become numb to violence and normalize it?*

Self-advertising was another surprise. Some men wore muscles the way businesses wear logos. Women emphasized curves, confidence, and sometimes reconstruction. Everyone seemed to present a résumé, even while ordering coffee. In America, if you don't promote yourself 24/7, you're ignored. Consumer society demands constant performance. Years later, social media would make things even worse. Being in business mode was survival here.

I met a divorced woman at the University of Vermont. She was friendly, forward, and eager — as if interviewing me for a position. She divorced her husband, she said, because he failed his exams. "I need someone with a future," she added plainly. I wanted to ask, *did you ever love him?* Instead, I kept silent and kept listening. The lesson was clear: in America, value is measured. If you don't perform as expected, you'll be replaced.

At times, I felt like I'd fallen into a mythological country — half Hollywood, half frontier. People were polite — "please" and "thank you" came packaged with every sentence. Thank-you cards arrived after dinner which had never happened in Spain. In Spain, formality was considered excessive; friendship began with informality. I walked the streets of Burlington, hoping for a plaza, espresso, noise, and laughter. Instead, I found weak coffee served in large cups — a shy, diluted imitation of itself — and a place called Main Street but devoid of the people and noise, and promise of personal connections, I was used to in Spain. I finally gave up walking down Main Street when I realized this was a different country, with different customs. My expectations were misplaced.

Many Americans were educated and knowledgeable. Others believed the U.S. was the center of the universe and had little idea of the rest of the world. Their questions came with innocence, not malice:

"Is Seville in Mexico?"

"Do you have universities in Spain?"

"Have you ever fought a bull?"

Americans were fiercely patriotic, and I quickly learned not to criticize the country, or else they would quickly say, "Then, why don't you just go back to where you came from?"

The fixation on race, last name, and country of origin surprised me. I sensed invisible castes. I learned to develop what W.E.B. Du Bois once called a double consciousness, seeing myself through others' eyes, while keeping my own vision intact. Communication became armor. If your English failed, people assumed you had nothing to say or worse. The more I mastered the language, the more I felt my identity shifting. English made me think with precision. *Say what you mean, and mean what you say.* I learned that phrase contains the whole key to survival.

Even at work, boundaries were both present but relaxed. A resident could sit with attendings or even department chairs. Hierarchy existed, but it didn't choke. It was possible to speak across ranks if you had something worth saying.

Still, I knew I had to tread carefully. Especially with politics. When asked about Vietnam, I said politely: "Europeans believe the war may not end well." I was lucky. Some foreign residents fled to Canada to avoid the draft. The U.S.

Army wanted to draft me. For some reason, they didn't. I stayed and finished my residency.

I learned that American freedom comes with the expectation of self-reliance. No one rushed in to save you. Advice arrived only if requested, and even then, I felt like I needed to know what kind of help to ask for. In Spain, dependence on family as a young adult was expected. In America, after eighteen, dependence was frowned upon. Freedom here was not a gift; it was a responsibility, and often a lonely one.

One day, I watched a father in Vermont fix his roof, his son proudly handing him tools. Not a contractor, not a handyman, just himself. In Spain, my father would have called a worker to hang a picture. Labor, he believed, diminished dignity. In America, labor seemed to define dignity. A man was judged not only by his profession, but by whether he could wield a hammer and fix a leaking pipe.

So I started learning.

I built things. Fixed what broke. Spoke up. Took risks. I learned about money and investing. Learned to defend my choices. Learned that if I didn't set boundaries, I would quietly become part of someone else's agenda.

That was perhaps my most important lesson of all: Freedom isn't just the ability to choose; it's the courage to live with the consequences of your decisions.

I had arrived in a land of optimism, possibilities, highways, skyscrapers, muscles, guns, and ambition.

But beneath it all, I sensed something else: America was a test. And I intended to pass it.

My First Boat Ride in Lake Champlain, Vermont, 1965

It was my first weekend in America. Vermont greeted me with an unexpected kindness of warm sunlight in late September, the kind the locals called Indian Summer. The air smelled faintly of pine and woodsmoke, and the sky above Lake Champlain was an impossible blue, a sky that felt somehow wider than any I had known in Europe.

My fellow psychiatry residents had invited me on a boat ride which was a casual gesture, perhaps, but to me felt like a rite of passage into this strange and luminous new world. I had never been on a boat like that. In Spain, Switzerland, and even England, life had always been more structured and restrained. Here, everything seemed looser and lighter. The lake stretched endlessly before us, cradled by distant green mountains. But it was the trees along the shoreline that stunned me most. They were ablaze, burning not with fire but with color. The hues of crimson, amber, gold, and deep emerald were so vivid that they felt unreal. I pointed at them, half-joking, half-serious.

"Are those trees sick?" I asked, genuinely puzzled.

My colleagues burst into laughter.

"No, no," one of them said, patting me on the back. "That's New England fall, my friend. We call it foliage. It's what people travel from all over the world to see."

"But it doesn't last," another added. "Soon the leaves will fall and cover the ground like a quilt. We enjoy it while we can."

That line, *enjoy it while we can*, lodged somewhere in me. It felt like a quiet truth about life itself.

Then, without ceremony, they all stripped to their trunks and bikinis and dove into the lake, one after the other. Their laughter bounced off the water like music. I sat there awkwardly, unsure of the etiquette. I hadn't brought a swimsuit. The boat's owner noticed my hesitation.

"Hey, since you're staying dry, why don't you take the wheel? Drive the boat a bit."

I looked at him, startled. "I've never driven a motorboat in my life."

He shrugged. "It's easy. Push the throttle forward, and it goes. Pull it back, and it stops." With that, he leapt into the water, leaving me alone on the deck with the steady hum of the engine.

I couldn't believe it. A total stranger had trusted me, a foreigner and a first-time sailor, with his boat. That would never happen in Spain. In Europe, everything had to be earned, certified, and approved. Here, there was something different. There was a willingness to trust.

At first, I did nothing. I just sat watching the swimmers splash and float. Then, curiously, that old inner friend of mine whispered, *why not?*

I placed my hand on the throttle and pushed gently. The boat lunged forward like a wild horse, skipping over the waves. The sudden speed took my breath away. Wind whipped against my face, my hair flew back, and for a moment, I felt like a boy again, free and alive.

The swimmers became tiny dots behind me. I panicked and steered back, laughing to myself, still high from the rush of power at my fingertips. When I returned, no one seemed angry. They just pulled themselves back onto the deck, water dripping from their skin, glowing in the sun, and began passing around baskets of sandwiches, potato chips, and lemonade. We ate in silence for a while, the kind of silence that occurs when everything feels too perfect to interrupt. The lake had gone still and reflected the trees like a mirror. For a moment I felt suspended between continents, between languages, between lives.

*

That weekend, I found myself at a dance in a rustic community hall near the hospital. One of the nurses was getting married the next day and had gathered her friends to celebrate her final night of freedom. I knew my language skills were still clumsy and the customs uncertain. I had dressed in a shirt and jacket which was probably too formal for the occasion. The music pounded through the wooden floorboards and beer foamed in plastic cups. Someone handed me one even though I didn't particularly want it.

Before long, the bride-to-be found me. Her smile carried a playful mischief as she pulled me onto the dance floor. Without hesitation, she pressed her body against mine, swaying boldly to the music. I froze, caught off guard. In Spain, flirtation had its rituals: a glance, a gesture, a slow unfolding. Here it was different: direct, unapologetic, immediate.

I laughed nervously and stepped back. She tried again. I slipped aside, gently but firmly. At last, she moved on unbothered, and her attention shifted to someone else. I stood there, both relieved and amused. It felt less like a test of masculinity than a test of restraint. At that moment, I understood that freedom in this new world meant more than opportunity; it also meant navigating choices without a script, careful not to mistake boldness for invitation or silence for consent.

Later that night, lying in my narrow dormitory bed, I stared at the ceiling while the music from the dance still pulsed faintly in my ears. I felt strangely divided, both full and hollow at once. Full of the beauty, the unexpected kindness, the newness of it all. Hollow from the familiar ache of distance, that quiet reminder that home was an ocean away.

Switzerland, France, and England each had carried its own flavor of Europe, bound by formality, history, and a touch of melancholy. But America was something altogether different. Brighter. Louder. Reckless, even. People here seemed to care less about lineage or tradition and more about what you could do, how you performed. They wanted heroes. They wanted to be dazzled. You were always being watched, measured, evaluated.

It didn't remind me of home. If anything, it reminded me just how far I had traveled from it. And yet, as I drifted toward sleep, I thought of Doris Day again:"Que será, será, whatever will be, will be."

My First Consultation, 1965

I was at Mary Fletcher Hospital, one of the teaching hospitals affiliated with the University of Vermont. I had entered the complex machinery of American medicine, and everything still felt slightly out of sync.

Morning staff meetings were a blur of clipped English, medical jargon, and inside references I didn't fully understand. But I learned quickly how to nod with conviction, grasp the gist, and stay just beneath the radar of the attendings and the ever-watchful nursing staff. Enough, it seemed, to earn a bit of trust. Or perhaps they were just desperate. My psychiatric experience from Spain, Switzerland, and England gave me an edge. I was sent off alone for my first official psychiatric consultation.

The request had come from a medical team in another part of the hospital. The patient, I was told, was an older woman in a state of agitation. That was all the information I got.

I found her sitting in a small conference room, one of those ominous spaces with a long wooden table and a sense of forgotten purpose. She was alone, quiet now, sipping slowly from a large, heavy, hospital-issued ceramic mug filled with coffee. Her hands were wrapped around it as if it contained something sacred.

I sat down across from her, careful not to make sudden movements. I offered a warm smile and said gently, "Good morning." No reply.

I tried again, softer this time: "How are you? How are you feeling today?"

She turned her head toward me with the slow motion of a puppet detached from its strings.

And then, I saw it.

Her face, though elderly, was etched with something much older. She had a look not of confusion, nor sorrow, but something primal. There was a deep, pensive malice behind her eyes, as if some dark current of rage had quietly risen from the depths and taken hold. It felt like hatred not just of me but of the world itself. A possession. A haunting.

Before I could blink, her hand shot through the air. The heavy ceramic mug, once cradled so gently, flew toward my head with violent precision. She threw it with force no one her age should still possess.

I ducked just in time.

The mug shattered against the tile floor behind me, sending coffee and ceramic shrapnel across the room. A pristine white floor tile was chipped and my pride, even more.

I sat there stunned. *Welcome to psychiatry*, I thought. *This is not a profession for the faint of heart.*

Still recovering from the jolt, I called for assistance. Orderlies arrived swiftly and with the practiced choreography of hospital protocol, she was gently restrained. I ordered an intramuscular injection of Haldol.

And as quickly as the storm had come, it passed. The fury dissolved. Her face softened and eyes dulled. The evil spirit, whatever it was, had taken its leave, at least for now.

I walked back down the corridor, feeling both disbelief and a sense of reverence. There was something sacred and dangerous about this work. I knew, even then, I was entering a world unlike any other where souls burst forth, disappear, and come back — where that evil darkness has a name, a diagnosis, and I would have the knowledge to make things better.

Skyscrapers of Wonder and Warning

The first time I stood on the streets of Manhattan and gazed upward was in 1966. I felt as if I had stepped into the very psyche of America, a place where dreams are engineered in steel, poured into concrete, and stretched skyward with unblinking confidence. I had seen majestic cities before. I had wandered the manicured avenues of Paris, the stately grandeur of London, the ancient weight of Rome, but nothing prepared me for the vertical audacity of New York City.

There, on the island that pulses with ambition, the buildings do not merely scrape the sky, they pierce it. Skyscrapers rise not just as structures but as symbols: of relentless drive, of defiant optimism, of a civilization that dared to believe it could master both gravity and fate. As I stood below those towers, neck craned and spine stretched, I found myself slowly turning in place like a sun-dazed pilgrim before cathedrals made not of stone but of industry and intention. My neck, quite literally, ached with awe.

From street level, the towers twisted my perspective. From above, like from a hotel room peering into a cavernous atrium, the effect was dizzying. It was as if the earth itself had opened and gravity reversed its pull, uncertain whether the emptiness below would swallow or awaken me. Either way, I was reminded how small I was, and how this city, this country, was immense.

Amid this commanding vertical display, I noticed the subtle erosion time inevitably brings. Some of these skyscrapers, once the crown jewels of modern civilization, wore wrinkles of age. The Art Deco grace of the Chrysler Building still dazzled, but its exterior bore the softened patina of memory. The Empire State Building remained iconic, but it, too, a relic of another era when greatness meant height and progress meant climbing.

More jarring still was the infrastructure at ground level. The highways circling the island like aging arteries were cracked and in constant need of repair. They, too, once spoke of a future imagined behind the wheel — speeding from borough to borough with streamlined efficiency — but revealed another truth, whispered in cones and barricades and the tired sighs of commuters: even giants must be maintained.

As I observed this contrast, between the towering optimism of the skyline and the weary decay beneath, I couldn't help but think of the men and women who built this place. Many of them immigrants. Foreign laborers. Brown hands, black hands, sunburnt necks, fearless hearts. During the Great Depression, when fear blanketed the world, they riveted steel to steel on narrow beams a thousand feet in the air. They did not ask for glory, but they deserved it.

And so, the skyscrapers of New York are more than monuments to ambition. They are layered symbols of creation and decline, of pride and neglect, of what humanity can accomplish when united in vision, and what it risks when blinded by its own reflection.

I left Manhattan that first time changed. Not just impressed but reflective. These towers shout to the world: Look at what we've done! And the world listens and marvels. But behind the shine, behind the vertigo and the glory, I heard another whisper: take care, for all greatness must be tended. Power must be humbled. And the hands that build the future must not be discarded once the skyline is drawn.

My First American Car and Girlfriend, 1966

My first car in America wasn't just a vehicle; it was a decision. New to the country, trying to find my footing, I was surrounded by cars that looked like battleships on wheels. Enormous, gas-guzzling, chrome-plated beasts that seemed more suited for parades than everyday life.

When I found the Chevrolet Corvair, it felt familiar. It was compact, at least by American standards, and nimble, more like the European cars I was used to. It felt manageable. Economical. Sensible.

I lived to regret it.

The Corvair was a stylish but notoriously flawed 1960s car, but I didn't know that yet. Ralph Nader's "Unsafe at Any Speed" hadn't made its way onto my reading list. But I would soon learn what he meant.

The car was a disaster in a cleverly ingenious way.

It leaked oil. The rear suspension, that infamous swing-axle design, made turning feel like flipping a coin. It might hold the road. Or it might just give up and slide into the nearest ditch. And the heating system, bless it, pumped in warm air infused with exhaust fumes. I couldn't decide whether to open the windows or inhale deeply.

Then there was the crash.

My first American girlfriend, who was sweet, bright-eyed, and full of youthful confidence, was driving the Corvair one day, going around a curve. The car did what Corvairs do. It betrayed her. It spun, skidded, and crashed. Thank God, nothing happened to her. She walked away shaken but unharmed.

The car, on the other hand, was never quite the same and neither was I. That was the moment I stopped pretending the Corvair was quirky or misunderstood. It was just a bad car.

Still, it had been mine. This was my first taste of American independence on four wheels. Loud, leaky, unreliable, even dangerous, but mine.

Looking back now, I realize that buying the Corvair was like many of the decisions I made during those early days: well-meaning, hopeful, and influenced by a mix of practicality and naïveté.

It taught me a lesson in American engineering, youthful optimism, and perhaps even love. But mostly, it taught me to always double-check before making any big purchase. Nobody will tell you or warn you. You are on your own, and what you don't know will catch up with you.

*

Virginia, my first American girlfriend, was a striking blonde French-Canadian dental assistant with a smile that could both soothe and unsettle. Her mother, with a half-knowing glance, warned me that she had just escaped a rough relationship and needed kindness. I nodded, a little too solemnly, unaware of the lessons ahead. I soon discovered that American women were a different breed. Bold, witty, and disarmingly independent.

She hated my smoking. Her remedy wasn't scolding or nagging. Instead, she perfected a kind of playful ambush. I'd raise a cigarette to my lips, and suddenly she'd appear, swift as a ninja of nicotine reform, snatching it away with a victorious grin. She was merciless, but I understood her intent. Eventually, she won. I quit.

Virginia's life, like that car, soon veered into turbulence. Her boss, a muscular dentist battling multiple sclerosis, began making advances she didn't welcome. In those days, decades before #MeToo gave women a collective voice, choices were narrow, and jobs were scarce. So, she endured in silence. She stopped complaining, and became less and less available after work. I watched from the edges of her struggle, restless and insecure. Jealousy gnawed at me. One night I even toyed with the absurd idea of climbing the office wall to spy through a window, to "catch them." Sanity, fortunately, intervened. I turned away, both literally and symbolically. I realized I did not own her and that I did not have to marry her either.

Human relationships are complicated and often messy. I learned that jealousy is a prison and a poison that we create for ourselves. That real freedom demands inner labor, not external control. I learned that love does not equal possession, that not every romance is meant to last.

My First Trip to American Court

Trouble, as it often does, began with something small: a screwdriver, or rather, the absence of one.

In 1966, when my shiny new license plates for the Corvair arrived in the mail, I realized I had no way to attach them to my car. No tools. No Swiss Army knife. Nothing. So, I placed the plates carefully in the back seat of the Corvair, reasoning that any reasonable person, say, a police officer, would understand why they hadn't been affixed yet. I was wrong.

One sunny afternoon, stopped at a red light, an officer peered through my windshield, spotted the absence of plates, and waved me over with the solemnity of a man about to make my life unnecessarily complicated.

I explained, proudly, that the plates were right there. I displayed them like a magician producing a rabbit from a hat. *Voilà!*

The law, I assumed, would smile upon my honesty. Instead, I received a ticket and a date to appear in court.

The courtroom in Burlington, Vermont, was packed. A curious blend of humanity with flannel shirts, denim jackets, and a few trembling souls in their Sunday best. I stood at the back, clutching my notice like a schoolboy anticipating the headmaster's reprimand.

When my name was called, I stepped forward from the back.

"How do you plead?" the judge asked.

Plead? I blinked. *Like, beg?*

He offered three options: guilty, not guilty, or no contest. I stood suspended in the philosophical void between opposites. I felt guilty; I had the plates. Not guilty also felt wrong; they weren't attached. No contest, I thought, sounded pleasantly ambiguous like the Switzerland of legal pleas. Surely the judge would recognize my good faith.

Ah, the naïveté of the newcomer.

The gavel came down. "Guilty. Fine. Next."

Guilty? I had the plates, but I didn't have the tool. Did intent mean nothing in this country?

It was only later that I came to understand the harsh reality of the American judicial system, the adversarial model. Here, nuance is discouraged. It gets overshadowed by binary logic. Guilty or not. Fight or surrender. And no contest? A polite way of surrender, to plead guilty.

The next morning, I discovered that my mishap had been featured in the local newspaper. Burlington had nothing more important to report than a clueless foreigner pleading no contest over two aluminum plates and a missing screwdriver.

The headline might as well have read: MAN FOUND GUILTY FOR LACK OF SCREWDRIVER

Strangers chuckled. My colleagues teased me. I thought everybody was being so childish.

In America, justice is not a soft, deliberative thing shared among wise elders. It is fast and binary, favoring those who know how to utilize it effectively. In Spain, three judges might ponder the moral shades of your case. In the U.S., it's your word against theirs. And unless you understand the rules of the game, or hire someone who does, you're likely to lose.

The truth, I realized, is often the first casualty in the courtroom's show. What matters is not how things really are, but how they seem, along with the evidence you present. The one who speaks louder, faster, and with more confidence usually comes out on top.

I screwed in my plates that afternoon using a borrowed tool and a bruised ego. The Corvair, despite its faults, looked strangely proud, as if it had passed its first rite of passage into American life.

As for me, I had entered the peculiar cathedral of American legality and left humbled, wiser, and somehow both defeated and amused.

My First Winter

It began quietly, almost reverently.

One evening, as I looked out my small window in the residence hall, the sky darkened with a gentle mystery. Then, as if called by a higher power, snowflakes started to fall — delicate, slow, like feathers drifting from invisible angels' wings. I pressed my face to the glass. I had never seen snow fall before. Beyond the weather, it felt like a revelation.

By morning, Vermont had transformed. The familiar world was gone. In its place stood a white cathedral of silence and light. Trees had donned bridal gowns. Roofs wore soft caps of purity. Even the rusted cars along the curb looked like sculptures wrapped in sugar. It was as if a giant hand had shaken the sugar bowl of heaven over the earth.

I stepped outside and was instantly baptized in the cold. My eyelashes froze. My ears ached with an icy sharpness that made me question whether I'd wake up with both still attached. And yet, I was enchanted.

The enchantment lasted precisely one day.

Then night fell like a curse. The temperature plummeted, and what had been snow turned to ice. The once-magical sidewalks became polished deathtraps. I soon learned to walk like a monk crossing a frozen lake. People fell left and right. A casual stroll to the hospital became a treacherous expedition. I half expected someone to hand me a helmet and a liability waiver.

And then came the slush. The second act of winter. What had once been pristine white became a muddy cocktail of sand and salt. Snowplows roared through the streets like mechanical beasts, leaving enormous walls of dirty snow in their wake. My boots were never dry. My coat lost its shape. My romantic visions of winter had transformed into the harsh reality of gritty survival.

Winter held one final challenge for me: skiing.

Armed with a secondhand pair of skis and a paperback manual titled *Learn to Ski in 10 Easy Steps*, which I had not finished reading, I decided to conquer the slopes of Stowe. I had never skied before. But in the madness of youth and exile, caution has a quiet voice.

A charming, mischievous, and entirely untrustworthy fellow resident from Argentina offered to guide me through the process. He invited me up the mountain, promising to teach me the basics. What he didn't mention was that his idea of teaching was to abandon me at the summit.

As soon as our lift touched the top, he took off like an Olympic champion, carving S-shapes into the snow with elegance. I was left alone, blinking into the white abyss.

There was only one way down.

And so, I went. Skis wobbling, legs shaking like a newborn deer, I pointed myself downhill and let gravity take over. It was not skiing. It was a survival ballet. I fell. I stood up. I fell again. But slowly and clumsily, I began to glide, not with grace, but with grit. I was wet, bruised, and triumphant by the time I reached the bottom.

My Argentine friend clapped and laughed. I smiled. He thought it was a joke. I had made it a victory.

That night, as I limped home through slush and darkness, I whispered a quiet vow to Vermont: "You may be cold, but I will not let you freeze my spirit. I will learn to ski."

Dirty Secrets of Vermont

When I first arrived in Vermont, I picked up a local newspaper and read a small article that stopped me in my tracks. It said, more or less: A man was fatally shot in a hunting accident. The hunter gets a $50 fine.

I reread it, thinking I must have misunderstood. Fifty dollars? In Spain, if someone killed another person, even by accident, it meant courts, prison, and a heavy weight of shame. But here, in Vermont, it looked as if a human life could be reduced to the cost of a traffic ticket.

At the hospital, I asked my colleagues, almost in disbelief: "How can this be? A man dies, and the punishment is just fifty dollars?"

They laughed at my confusion. To them, it was apparent: guns were everywhere in America, especially in Vermont. You could buy them in a store like Walmart, at roadside fairs, or even through the mail. Nearly everyone owned a hunting rifle.

Every fall, the state issues licenses for deer hunting. For a few short weeks, the woods came alive with hunters carrying rifles slung over their shoulders and eyes scanning for movement. Pine, maple, and birch trees closed in thickly around them, their leaves turning fire-red and gold. In those woods lived unsuspecting deer, creeping through the brush, until suddenly they didn't. By Sunday evening, cars returned to town with deer carcasses tied to their trunks, blood dripping onto the road.

Sometimes what moved in the woods wasn't a deer but another hunter. One wrong twitch, one quick pull of a trigger, and a man was dead. But in Vermont, this was no scandal.

"Accidents happen," they told me. A fine was enough.

I was even invited to join hunting trips and urged to buy a rifle. But the thought made me uneasy. I had heard too many stories of hunters killing themselves by mistake or being shot by their friends.

Then there was the other ritual of Vermont winters: ice fishing. When Lake Champlain froze solid, from December to early March, people would drive their cars straight onto the ice, drill holes, and sit for hours waiting for a fish to bite. It was strange and beautiful; the frozen lake was dotted with little wooden shacks and bundled-up figures.

But this beauty had a dark side. Every year, as spring approached, the ice began to melt and sometimes faster than people realized. Every year, cars fell through and people too. The ice would crack under their weight, open for an instant, then close again, trapping them under the surface. Rescue was nearly impossible. Often, the would-be rescuers themselves drowned trying to save others. And still, it happened again the following year, as if the tragedies were just part of the cycle of seasons.

These were some of the hidden truths of Vermont: thick woods full of life and death, frozen lakes that promised both joy and peril. To an outsider like me, the place was achingly beautiful, but its beauty always carried a warning of caution. To be careful, or else you could die — just like that.

The Girl in the ICU

I was a young resident rotating through the Neurology Ward at DeGoesbriand Memorial Hospital in Burlington, Vermont. The place was full of the smell of bleach, along with the weight of fatigue and resignation. Hope lived there, but only in rationed doses, dispensed sparingly. I was determined to prove myself to the staff, to the system, and perhaps even to the lingering ghosts of my childhood hunger for approval. So, I arrived before dawn and stayed late, brushing by the hills as I left late into the night.

I lingered because there was something sacred in those rooms. Something wordless. Something that existed not in the charts or the rounds but in the silences in between.

One day, I noticed a new admission in the ICU. She was a young woman who was utterly paralyzed. Guillain-Barré Syndrome had locked her in her body that acts as a living tomb built by her own immune system. She could not speak. She could not even blink to signal her existence. She lay there like a statue. She was present but unreachable.

Most people passed her by. What could be done? There was no treatment to offer, no heroic intervention to justify the time. She was a case without a dialogue, a patient without a way to answer back. And so, she became invisible, reduced to a bed number and vital signs, a ghost among the living.

But I could not ignore her. Something in me refused.

I had nothing to offer. No unique cure or cleverness or unheard-of miracles. I gave her the only thing I had: presence. Each time I passed, I held her hand. I didn't speak much. I didn't expect acknowledgement. I wasn't even sure she knew I existed. Yet I kept holding her hand, gently and patiently, letting my touch act as a kind of silent prayer.

Weeks went by. My rotation ended. I left Vermont for Montreal, carrying with me new hospitals, new patients, and new urgencies. The girl receded into memory. She became one face in the vast sea of cases we are trained to let go.

Until one day when a package arrived.

The handwriting on the label meant nothing to me. Inside was a letter written deliberately. It was from her.

She had recovered.

Waterbury tracked me down. She remembered everything from my hand to my presence to the simple fact that I had not looked away when she was locked inside herself. She thanked me, not for curing her as I had done no such thing, but for something rarer. She thanked me for recognizing her humanity when the world had passed her by.

In the package was a pair of moccasins she had sewn by hand. They were soft, warm, and exquisitely crafted. When I slipped them on, they fit like a memory.

I wept.

In medicine, we are taught to measure value in terms of outcomes, efficiency, and things that can be billed, charted, or cured. This moment fits none of those categories. It was not recorded. It was not reimbursed.

It was not "productive." It was simply a human connection.

And it reminded me, as I always need reminding, that morality is not forged in grand gestures but in the smallest acts of care. In refusing to look away. In bearing witness. Even when all you have to offer is your presence.

Boston City Hospital, 1968

It was a crisp Saturday morning in early spring when I drove from Burlington, Vermont, to Boston, Massachusetts. I was a psychiatry resident at the University of Vermont, still young and wide-eyed, trying to find my place in a world that seemed to be unraveling. The Vietnam War was raging on the news, in the streets, and in the hearts and minds of every American. That morning, I was headed to Grand Rounds at Boston University, expecting clinical discussions and polished lectures.

What I didn't expect was horror. Two surgeons stood before the audience, dressed in immaculate military uniforms, their faces grim with experience. They had just returned from war in Vietnam and brought heavy cargo with them: hundreds of slides full of images of the wounded, the dying, and the destroyed.

As the lights dimmed and the first slide snapped onto the screen, the room fell silent. A soldier missing both legs, flesh torn and blackened. Another with his abdomen ripped open, intestines spilling onto a blood-soaked stretcher. Heads blown apart, eyes wide open in frozen terror, limbs twisted grotesquely. The images kept coming, one after another, relentless and raw.

I sat frozen in my chair, my stomach churning. I had seen injuries before, on-call shifts in the ER, and psychiatric evaluations of trauma patients, but nothing like this. This wasn't medicine. This was butchery on an industrial scale of suffering.

Something shifted in me that day. I knew I was up against new challenges I hadn't thought about before. And something told me this wouldn't be the last time I'd pay witness to atrocity.

Assassinations and Shock, 1968

Assassination of MLK Jr. on April 4

It had been another long, grueling day at the hospital in my residency.

I don't remember the cases, the rounds, or the faces I saw that day—just the fatigue that clung to my body like a second skin. I was running on fumes, as we all were, juggling life and death with too little sleep and too many questions.

I stepped into the hospital residence where the interns and residents lived. The communal living room was dimly lit and the television was already on. I didn't intend to watch anything. I only meant to sit for a moment and let the day's weight melt into the cushions.

What I saw on the screen felt impossible. Unthinkable. The country was on fire. The television footage jumped from city to city: New York, Philadelphia, Washington, D.C., Chicago, Los Angeles, Detroit. One after another, flames lit up the screen like scenes from a war zone. Sirens wailed, storefronts shattered, people ran. The camera panned across broken glass, flaming storefronts, and lines of riot police braced behind shields. It felt like the country was tearing itself apart in real time right there on our small black-and-white TV.

I stared, trying to make sense of the chaos. It felt surreal, like watching a nightmare. The news came through: Martin Luther King Jr. had been assassinated.

The breath left my lungs. The room went even quieter than it already was. Martin Luther King Jr., a voice for peace and nonviolence, was murdered in Memphis. And in the wake of his death, the country was unraveling.

I sat frozen on the couch, unable to move.

The news anchors called it "rioting." They talked about "violence in the streets." But what I saw on the screen, what I felt in my gut, was something more profound. It was grief. It was rage. It was the scream of a people who had reached the edge of endurance.

They were burning their own neighborhoods. At first, that made no sense to me. *Why destroy what you have?* But then I began to understand. This was not strategic destruction. It was a desperate sorrow made visible. It was the unbearable pain of being unheard decade after decade that finally erupted into flames.

I was a newcomer to this country. I had not grown up with its racial fault lines, its history of slavery and segregation, of civil rights and police batons. I was learning it all in real time and that night I saw it laid bare in flames.

America was breaking open.

I was still learning its rhythms, promises, and betrayals. I stood there silent and stunned. I had known America as a land of opportunity, progress, and democracy but nothing in my upbringing had prepared me for this night. I had never seen a society so profoundly fractured.

I remember thinking: *this is not just a moment of crisis, it's a reckoning. A wound long in the making is finally breaking open.*

The room remained quiet. None of us had the words. We were doctors-in-training but no amount of education could help us make sense of the collective trauma we were witnessing.

I knew this country was hurting in ways I had never imagined and now I was a part of it.

Assassination of Bobby Kennedy on June 6

I was still in the hospital residency when the news broke on TV that Robert Francis Kennedy (RFK, or Bobby) had been shot at the Ambassador Hotel in Los Angeles following his victory speech. After leaving the podium, he tried to exit through a kitchen hallway where he was shot multiple times by Sirhan Sirhan, reportedly in retaliation for Kennedy's support of Israel during the Six-Day War. He died just after midnight.

Bobby had announced his candidacy for president earlier that year. Over a year earlier, he had called for a halt to U.S. bombing in Vietnam. Before his death, he had also expressed strong support for a bill to abolish the death penalty in the United States.

I had hoped he would be elected President of the United States, continuing his brother's work. Tragically, he died at Good Samaritan Hospital in Los Angeles nearly twenty-five hours after he was shot. He was buried at Arlington National Cemetery.

I remember watching the news of his brother's assassination, the death of President John F. Kennedy, on TV while I was still living in Spain. I couldn't believe the way the alleged assassin, Oswald, was himself assassinated– shot in front of police officers, journalists, and the world, while being transferred to another location. It was hard to believe the authorities had been so lax as to allow a crowd to gather around someone so critical to the investigation.

Four major political assassinations occurred in the U.S. during the 1960s: John F. Kennedy in 1963, Malcolm X in 1965, Martin Luther King Jr. in April 1968, and Robert F. Kennedy in June 1968.

I felt emotionally numb. I couldn't believe so many tragedies could occur in such a short time in this country. I was starting to see different sides of America. Starting to recognize how my work and how I approached it might be shifting with the world around me.

Waterbury and the Unfinished Promise of Community Care

In the 1970s, Waterbury, Vermont, felt like a town caught between eras. Some factories had closed. Many houses looked tired. The largest employer left was the state hospital.

Waterbury State Hospital sat at the edge of town in an old red-brick complex that looked permanent and calm from the outside. Inside, it was a different world. During my residency at the University of Vermont, I completed a three-month rotation. I entered as a physician-in-training to treat patients but also to learn how the system worked.

The hospital depended on local workers and on foreign-born doctors. Many psychiatrists were recruited from abroad and were offered housing and other benefits. Few American-born psychiatrists chose to work there unless they held high administrative roles. In practice, the nursing staff managed the hospital's daily operations. The doctors came and went. The institution had its own momentum.

At first glance, the campus looked orderly. The lawns were kept. The staff housing looked uniform. I was told patients did much of the maintenance. It sounded efficient. It also sounded like a warning.

Inside, the building felt designed for control. The corridors were long. The light was dim. The air smelled of disinfectant and damp clothing. Keys jingled. Doors slammed. The routines were rigid. I felt, in my body, that this place was built to contain people, not to restore them.

One unit has stayed with me. It housed severely ill chronic schizophrenic patients, many incontinent and unable to care for themselves. Each morning, they were bathed together in a special room and hosed down in groups. Staff described it as efficient. What I saw was mass bathing on an industrial scale. Thin naked bodies. Little privacy. Little dignity. The image shook me. It reminded me, in the worst way, of photographs from the Holocaust — human beings reduced to objects to be processed.

It is tempting to blame individuals for what happens in places like that. Sometimes staff behaved harshly. Sometimes they looked numb. But I learned something important at Waterbury: the institution shapes the people inside it. The environment trains you. The routine trains you. The hierarchy trains you.

I had read about Philip Zimbardo's Stanford Prison Study and Stanley Milgram's obedience experiments. Waterbury made those lessons feel real. Not because the staff were monsters, but because ordinary people can be pulled toward indifference and routine obedience when the system rewards compliance and punishes hesitation. Patients, in turn, adapt by submitting, resisting, withdrawing, or breaking down. The roles harden. Everyone becomes smaller.

I remember one nurse handing medication to a patient. Her voice dropped. She glanced over her shoulder and said, almost as a confession, "I know this place is not what it should be." That sentence mattered to me. It indicated to me that she still had a moral compass. It also told me she felt trapped.

I left Waterbury with grief and anger, but also with clarity. The problem was not one tired nurse or one rough attendant. The problem was a model of care that had become too large, too closed, and too resistant to change. The state hospital system was established for public purposes, but over the decades, it drifted toward custodial care. Order mattered more than treatment. Efficiency mattered more than empathy. And once those values take over, cruelty can appear without anyone naming it. By then, the old system was already beginning to collapse.

The country was moving toward deinstitutionalization and community care. President John F. Kennedy signed the Community Mental Health Act in 1963. The promise was bold: shift treatment from massive state hospitals to community mental health centers rooted in local neighborhoods. The timing also fit the science. New medications changed what was possible. Chlorpromazine helped many people with psychosis. Imipramine helped many with depression. Lithium helped many with bipolar disorder. Between the 1950s and the 1990s, the population of state hospitals fell dramatically — often described as a drop of about 95%. In theory, many people who had been locked away could now live outside hospital walls. The idea was humane but the execution was not.

Community care required funding, housing, staffing, and long-term follow-up. In many places, those supports did not arrive at a large enough scale. Hospitals emptied faster than communities prepared. The result was not liberation. It was displacement.

Over time, I watched the same patients cycle through new forms of abandonment. Some became homeless. Some lived in shelters and were repeatedly traumatized. Some refused treatment, not out of stubbornness, but because their illness robbed them of insight and trust. Others ended up in jail. The prison system became a crude substitute for the hospital system, with officers and courts trying to manage psychosis with handcuffs and isolation.

This is one of the hardest truths in psychiatry: the people most in need are often least able to ask for help. When laws and systems treat refusal as "choice," we can end up protecting autonomy in theory while abandoning human beings in practice.

I also saw how law, medicine, and policy sometimes worked at cross-purposes. In my view, the way some statutes are written and applied —such as involuntary treatment standards and privacy rules — can make it harder to intervene early and protect people who cannot recognize their own illness. Families are often dismissed until the situation becomes a crisis. By the time the system acts, damage has already been done.

I do not say this lightly. Civil liberties matter. History provides many reasons to fear the abuse of power. But there is also a quiet cruelty in leaving a psychotic person to deteriorate on the street because "they have rights," while offering no realistic path to treatment, housing, and sustained care. A broken leg is visible. A broken mind is not. The disability can be just as real, and the consequences spread through families and communities.

And still, I do not tell this story as pure despair.

Even in bad systems, there are good people. I have met them everywhere. Nurses who protect patients in small ways. Clinicians who keep showing up. Outreach teams who sit patiently with someone who distrusts everyone. Judges who support mental health courts. Sheriffs and officers are learning de-escalation and treatment options. Advocacy groups like NAMI are pushing the public to see the truth that many prefer to ignore.

I remember working with a mobile outreach team in New York City. We visited individuals who were too paranoid to keep clinic appointments. Sometimes they called the police on us before we entered the building. If we were allowed in, we sat on worn couches and spoke slowly, trying to earn a few minutes of trust. When medication was needed, we used it carefully. When long-acting injectable antipsychotics made sense, we offered them with restraint and respect, mindful of side effects. Sometimes the change was striking. At the next visit, the muttering stopped. The paranoia and fear had improved or gone. A person returned to being themselves. Those moments sustained me.

Waterbury taught me what institutions can do to human beings when care becomes custody. The community mental health movement taught me what happens when ideals are launched without sufficient structure and budgets to sustain them. The lesson from both is the same: the chronically mentally ill cannot be treated as a political inconvenience or a budget line. They require sustained, realistic care — medical, social, and legal — built for the long haul. Societies can be judged by how well they treat people who can't manage their lives or care for themselves.

Things may be better than they were, but I am not sure. I know many families experiencing extreme suffering because they cannot access mental health care for their loved one in a system too complicated for people to understand. I believe local, state, and federal governments have a responsibility to care for disabled people who cannot care for themselves. Not as charity. As a basic duty of a decent society. If we want fewer tragedies, fewer jails functioning as hospitals, and fewer families living in despair, we will need better funding, better mental health laws, better coordination, greater commitment, and moral determination from those who have the power to effect these improvements. Mental health professionals have the duty to inform society of what's going on and how to improve the system.

And since Waterbury, I knew I wanted to be part of that work.

Kindness of Strangers

I had finished my psychiatric residency at the University of Vermont and passed the state board exam. New York was next and I had a fellowship lined up in Psychiatric Research at Downstate Medical Center. But there was one final obstacle: a license. Not just a flimsy hospital badge but a state license to practice medicine in the United States.

Not having this license meant no fellowship. No future.

Everything rode on that exam.

I had prepared obsessively. Even though I was unfamiliar with the term "ADHD," I was aware of my brain's ability, or difficulty, to manage time. I trained like an Olympian with timed drills, full practice exams, and ruthless discipline. I could hit the required 75 percent, even beat it. But only if everything lined up with no distractions nor panic.

Of course, panic has a wicked sense of timing.

The testing room was packed, humming with nervous silence. Chairs creaked. Papers rustled. The proctor gave the signal, and the air thickened with tension. I bent over the exam and dove in.

For the first hour, I kept pace. But then cracks appeared. A cough from the corner. A pencil dropping. A chair scraping against the floor. Each sound yanked me off track. I reeled myself back repeatedly, but the rhythm was gone.

And then, the real torture. People began leaving.

One by one, confident young doctors stood, handed in their papers, and strode out with the swagger of winners. Meanwhile, I was drowning somewhere around question 185. Fifteen more to go. My pulse roared in my ears. I fought the panic, but it slipped its leash.

"Time is up," the proctor called. "Hand in your answer sheets."

I stared at mine. Ten blank questions. Ten. My hands went cold. My throat closed. The proctor's shoes clicked toward me. He extended his hand.

Something inside me snapped.

I stood, tore the answer sheet in half, and thrust the pieces at him.

He blinked. "What are you doing?"

"I need to speak to the exam manager," I said. My voice came out calm, almost detached, as if someone else were speaking.

I walked out before he could argue and asked to see the person in charge.

An older man appeared who carried himself in a measured and unhurried manner with the kind of eyes that had seen too many desperate stories to flinch. He invited me to sit.

I told him everything. I informed him about the preparation, the timing, and the questions that were left blank. I wasn't pleading. I wasn't making excuses. I was simply laying down the truth. I hadn't failed out of laziness or ignorance. I just hadn't been fast enough.

He listened without interrupting. Finally, he exhaled and leaned back. "I can justify a missing answer sheet," he said quietly. "Why don't you come back this afternoon and retake the test?"

For a moment, I couldn't move. Did I hear him right? The world paused.

"Yes," I managed, my voice breaking. "Yes, thank you. Thank you."

After lunch, I returned to a new room with a fresh group of doctors. The same exam waited for me, but this time, fear had no claws. I moved from question to question with steady hands. I knew the terrain.

I finished first and walked out into the afternoon light knowing I'd passed.

I never saw that man again. Never got to shake his hand, buy him dinner, tell him what his kindness had meant. Maybe that was better. Maybe his act didn't require repayment.

Carl Jung said, "Every individual is an exception to the rule." When people insist that, "We must always follow the rules," I cringe. I know what that really means: someone, somewhere, who deserves an exception, will suffer.

I say, we should follow the rules, but sometimes we must ignore them to do the right thing.

I remember him still. His mercy turned a rigid system into something just. He bent the rules not to favor me but simply to make the world a little fairer. I remember the stranger who chose compassion over protocol and how his choice opened the door to my future.

Chapter 8: Canada and Fieldwork

"One of the most effective ways to learn about oneself is by taking seriously the cultures of others. It forces you to pay attention to those details of life that differentiate them from you."

— Edward T. Hall, *The Silent Language*

Montreal Children's Hospital and McGill University, 1968-69

Montreal welcomed me with its contradictions: icy winters that drove me underground into the vast, cathedral-like tunnels of the metro, and summers that burst with outdoor cafés, jazz in the streets, and the taste of ripe fruit that seemed to carry the warmth of Europe across the Atlantic. For a year, McGill University became my refuge, my laboratory, and my window into the ways culture shapes the mind.

My first stay in Montreal lasted three months. I was doing a rotation in Child Psychiatry at the Montreal Children's Hospital, and I remember it clearly because that summer an outbreak of Hepatitis A swept through the hospital. It was a nosocomial epidemic — meaning it was spreading inside the hospital itself. Because of it, the psychiatric unit stopped taking new admissions. Only a few children were left in the ward. The ones who stayed had already learned how to keep people away. They smeared their feces on walls, windows, and doors.

A female psychiatric resident was supposed to join me, but she was pregnant and excused. Attendees were rarely present. In practice, I was alone with a few nurses, managing a ward of angry, frightened kids — kids who had learned that the best defense was causing disgust, to keep the grown-ups away.

People later said I was "brave" and a "good therapist." I wasn't. I was just curious — and too young to be afraid. Strangely, I enjoyed the challenge. The teenagers eventually warmed up to me because they thought I was a mysterious American from Vermont. That simple misunderstanding helped. Canadian teenagers admired Americans. They began to share their stories with me and in return, I taught them boundaries. Not from textbooks but from lived moments.

The nurses had mostly given up on discipline. Their laissez-faire approach meant the teenagers ran the unit. I enforced the no-smoking rule firmly and that alone made them see me differently. Respect sometimes begins when someone says no and means it. The child psychiatry rotation taught me things no classroom could, especially when there was no supervision. I washed my hands carefully every time I entered or left the unit. And no, I never got Hepatitis A.

One Friday morning, we gathered in the hospital theater for Grand Rounds. The guest speaker was Dr. Thomas Szasz, a famous and controversial figure in psychiatry. He debated a Canadian psychiatrist about whether involuntary treatment is ethical. Szasz defended the same ideas he had promoted since his 1961 book *The Myth of Mental Illness*: mental illness is not a medical disease but a metaphor for the struggles of living — and psychiatry, he argued, functions as a tool of social control.

According to him, labeling unwanted behavior as "mental illness" lets people avoid responsibility — and civil commitment becomes a way to take away their fundamental civil freedoms in the name of treatment. He stood firmly with the anti-psychiatry movement, a group that challenged the very foundation of psychiatric practice.

He was not alone in those ideas. The French philosopher Michel Foucault, author of *Madness and Civilization*, traced how Western societies shifted over centuries. In the Middle Ages, "fools" wandered city streets freely. Later, asylums were built, and walls went up. The "insane" were removed from sight and from society. Madness was redefined — not cured, but contained.

At the end of the debate, the audience was asked to vote. Most disagreed with Dr. Szasz — and so did I. Not because his ideas lacked merit, but because reality often makes theory bow its head.

Sometimes patients are out of control — aggressive, unaware, and unwilling to accept help. Sometimes families are terrified. Someone must act. And in those moments, psychiatrists must step forward — not because they want control but because no one else knows what to do.

Szasz and Foucault were right to challenge the system. Their questions were important. But theory exists in still water. Real life moves like a river. Sometimes it floods.

I'm reminded of Ludwig Wittgenstein, who said, "Words have meaning only in the stream of life." He believed philosophy should help us find a way out of the "fly-bottle"— the trap that thinkers create when they forget that words and theories must stay connected to real life, real people, real situations.

That summer in Montreal, I met children who weren't cases, diagnoses, or philosophical puzzles. They were confused, wounded human beings trying to defend themselves. That doesn't fit neatly into theory, but it fits perfectly into life. And life, not theory, is where healing must begin.

*

Next, I was accepted as a Fellow in Transcultural Psychiatry at McGill University, a field barely known at the time. I was soon asked to teach medical students how culture weaves itself into every diagnosis, every gesture, every silence between doctor and patient. One afternoon, I stood before a sea of young faces in a lecture hall that seemed too large for one voice. Hundreds of students sat quietly, their curiosity piqued, ready to learn.

I began with stories. "Imagine," I told them, "A patient who hears voices. In Vermont, he might be diagnosed with schizophrenia. In Nigeria, he may be considered a prophet. The symptom is the same, but the meaning, the very soul of it, depends on where you stand."

Beside me was a young American anthropologist, animated and sharp. He spoke with his hands, his body alive as he showed them how a shrug, a glance, a pause in speech can speak louder than any stethoscope. Together, we wove a simple truth: healing begins not with pills or scalpels but with listening. Listening in the language of another's world.

I could see the students leaning in, not because I was offering dogma but because I was opening a door they hadn't known existed. Cultural literacy in medicine — what a strange, radical idea then. But how could one treat the body without also honoring the culture that carries it? To feel understood, I reminded them, is already a form of healing.

When winter's grip grew too sharp, I descended into Montreal's underground city, a maze of warmth where I could walk for miles beneath the ice. In summer, I emerged again to cafés where the air smelled of strong coffee and butter, where conversations floated between French and English, and where, for a moment, I felt I belonged everywhere and nowhere.

It was then that the world beckoned louder. With the guidance of a mentor, I set out to design questionnaires to use in field research that would take me far beyond Montreal. I was no longer just a doctor. I was becoming a wayfarer of the human spirit, wandering between cultures to ask the oldest question medicine has ever faced: how to understand the person and the culture that shaped him before we try to heal.

Jamaica, West Indies, 1969

The whole world held its breath. America had set its gaze skyward, aiming for the impossible: a man on the moon. You could feel the buzz of it, even on Kingston's warm, humid streets. Radios crackled in shops and cafés. People gathered around old televisions with flickering black-and-white screens, straining to catch images of the lunar module descending on a world that no one had ever touched.

I was in Jamaica, not Queens, but the West Indies. I had come not as a tourist, but as a young doctor, completing my research for McGill. I was curious and concerned about the unseen gravity pulling at the lives of Jamaican youth. I was there to study adolescents with absent fathers and how the gaps shaped the psyche, how the silence of a missing man could echo louder than his voice.

Jamaica was a living laboratory for this kind of work. The fabric of many families was woven without the thread of a father. Women raised children with resilience and grace, but often alone. It was not uncommon for one woman to have children by two, three, even four different men. These men, some present in spirit, some vanished entirely, would leave for far-off places to find work: England, the United States, the oil fields of Venezuela. Some sent money back; others sent silence.

They called them baby-mothers, a term loaded with complexity and spoken with both affection and resignation. The phrase held everything: love, survival, betrayal, and pride.

Amid the absence, there was vitality. Jamaican youth were vibrant, quick-witted, and alert to the world around them. They laughed easily, danced instinctively. But underneath that rhythm, you could sense a searching, a question: "Where is he?" Not always spoken aloud but present in the corners of their lives, like an unfinished sentence.

As Americans were landing on the moon, planting flags on the lunar surface, I was sitting in a modest Kingston school, talking to a boy who hadn't seen his father in seven years. He looked up at me with eyes that had already learned not to expect too much. "He's gone foreign," he said, and shrugged.

Gone foreign.

It struck me as strange, how a world that could reach the stars still left so many boys unable to get their fathers.

The moonshot was a miracle of science, ambition, and belief. But down here on Earth, we had our own miracles to attempt: rebuilding families, restoring dignity, offering a hand to boys learning how to become men without a model.

That contrast between the cosmic and the intimate, between the headlines and the hidden lives, shaped something in me. The world was advancing, but healing human hearts was slower work: quieter and more fragile.

In Jamaica, I was reminded that the most incredible distances aren't always measured in miles but in absence.

The Mayas, Yucatán, 1969

The rhythms of the lush island of Jamaica were still pulsing through me when I arrived in the Yucatán Peninsula. I flew west and landed in Mérida, the capital, drawn not by reason but by quiet intuition, a whisper I couldn't name. The city welcomed me with the soft chaos of its heat and color. A taxi took me from the airport into the heart of Mérida, and through the window, I watched a place that felt both foreign and oddly familiar unfold.

I had asked not for luxury but for something simple. "No expensive hotels," I had said. And they listened, but perhaps too well. The hotel they brought me to was worn down. The walls sagged; the furniture bore the weight of time and neglect. It was too much for me, someone who never minded humble places. I couldn't stay. I needed something else, something cleaner, quieter, and more alive.

The streets outside told a different story, one of life, texture, and spirit. The people moved slowly in the midday sun, dressed in wide, white pants and loose, cotton shirts, with straw hats shading their faces. There was a raw beauty in how they carried themselves, with simplicity and pride.

Everywhere, food vendors lined the streets. The smell of tortillas sizzling on open griddles, of empanadas frying golden in oil, and of beans thick, seasoned, and earthy rose in aromatic waves. It was more than a smell; it was a language, a kind of music.

There was warmth in how strangers looked at me. I felt welcome, even as a foreigner. I felt held by something ancient, reminiscent of a bygone era, perhaps colonial times.

And then, as if guided by grace, I remembered her, Heather, the young Canadian anthropologist I had met back in Montreal during those years shaped by intellect and winter. She had worked at McGill, where thoughts ran deep and silence was often more eloquent than speech. Heather was quiet but not in a hollow way. She listened with her whole being. I remembered her eyes, which seemed to dwell beneath the surface of things.

She had moved to Mérida, drawn by ancient echoes. She came to study the sacred myths, the ruins that time had not yet silenced. When I reached out, she responded quickly, telling me I could stay with her.

Her home was not a house in the usual sense, it was a Mexican compound with thick walls and an expansive courtyard where bougainvillea spilled over stone and birds flitted in and out of the shade. Books were stacked on every surface, the scent of ink and aged paper mixing with the jasmine that bloomed by the open windows.

With Heather's guidance, Mérida's strangeness began to soften. She showed me more than streets and ruins; she showed me a way of being there. She introduced me to the rhythms of local life and how *curanderos*, the traditional healers, spoke of illness not just as a physical affliction but as a disturbance of harmony. We discussed the sacred geometry of the Mayan temples, the ancient science still hidden within their stones. She shared pieces of her research for McGill, and I shared the questions I had carried silently for years — about the body, the soul, and the invisible threads that bind them.

Heather's Spanish was serviceable, lightly brushed with her foreign accent, charmingly imperfect. Mine flowed more freely, and together we navigated the layers of language and meaning that made Mérida what it was.

Through her, I met Emiliano, a local physician with warm eyes and an easy, grounded presence. He specialized in gastrointestinal issues, but there was nothing clinical about his spirit. He was an Indigenous man, proud of his roots and deeply connected to his heritage. There was something timeless in the way he moved through the world, as though he were carrying his ancestors with him.

We became fast friends. He spoke to me not just as a fellow doctor, but as a brother. One afternoon, he invited me to lunch at his mother's house. The invitation came late, and I had already eaten, but I went anyway. Something told me the visit mattered more than the food.

*

The house was large, warm, and full of earthy scent and sunlight. When we arrived, he introduced me to his mother, a regal woman with sharp, wise eyes. Out of instinct or reverence, I took her hand and kissed it, as though I were greeting a Mayan queen. She smiled at me with amused approval, and I think she liked that gesture. It crossed the boundaries of custom and time.

Then I saw the table.

It was covered, overflowing, with food. Dozens of small, intricate dishes, each one prepared with evident care and pride. It was like a landscape of flavor I had never seen before. I was full but tasted what I could. Every bite was a revelation. It reminded me of Spanish tapas, but wilder, earthier, and more ancient. Each dish seemed to carry a story.

Before we left, I retook Emiliano's mother's hand, this time not as a gesture of gallantry but of proper reverence. I thanked her from the bottom of my heart for her kindness, her warmth, and the astonishing delicacies she had prepared in honor of her son's guest. She had cooked not just a meal but a welcome and offering of love in the language of spices and texture.

That moment stayed with me. It reminded me that sometimes the most sacred acts are simple: a hand kissed, a plate offered, a smile exchanged. In those small rituals, life breathes its oldest truths.

*

Not long after, Emiliano surprised me.

He told me he had planned a visit, something special, something not easily found on maps. A meeting with a *curandero*.

We drove for hours, leaving the paved world behind. The road grew narrower, the trees wilder, the sky larger and emptier.

At the road's end, we parked beside a stretch of tall grass and walked. The heat pressed down as we made our way across the fields. There was no sign of life until we saw a small cottage with the *curandero,* standing still, beside it.

He was there waiting for us.

The *curandero* stood tall. His face bore a northern quality, his features sharp, weathered, and strangely European. I had heard stories, whispers of Norwegians or other seafarers who may have landed on these coasts centuries ago. *Could he be a descendant of those early wanderers? Or was it just one of those faces born from mystery, as if shaped by the wind and sky alone?*

Emiliano leaned toward me as we approached and spoke quietly telling me I was to give him money. I hadn't been told beforehand, and the request caught me off guard. I reached into my pocket and found a single bill, a twenty-dollar note that was crumpled but clean.

The *curandero* received it without emotion, as if the act, not the amount, mattered. He nodded once, gravely, but looked at me with eyes that seemed to see both the surface and what lay behind it.

"You may ask me anything," he said in Spanish. His voice was quiet but solid.

For a moment, I didn't know what to say. The air around us felt heavier now, like the boundary between worlds had thinned. I thought about it, then asked: "What is my path? What am I meant to do in this life?"

The question rose from somewhere deep within me, not rehearsed, not intellectual. It was the question that speaks for itself before you even understand it. I had been carrying it. And here, in this open field, under the weightless sky, I had finally placed it at someone's feet.

The *curandero* didn't answer right away. He looked at me for a long moment, not unkindly, but as though weighing something more than my words. Then he motioned for us to sit. The three of us sat in a triangle in the dry grass.

"You are a healer," he said, "but not just of the body. Your hands know medicine, yes. But your heart carries other work."

I felt something stir in me. Recognition, perhaps, or fear. He spoke slowly, with pauses that allowed the land to listen.

"You have traveled far, but you are still wandering. Your medicine will not be found in hospitals alone. It will come from people, their stories, and your willingness to be open and vulnerable. That is your way."

He fell silent again. Then, after a moment, he added, "There is a woman who will walk with you. She is not beside you yet. But she is coming. And she will know you when you do not even know yourself."

We drove back to Mérida in near-total silence. I felt in awe. I was a Western-trained psychiatrist, but at that moment, I felt like an apprentice in an unknown world.

The road was long and familiar now, but it felt changed somehow. Or maybe we were the ones transformed. Emiliano kept his eyes on the road, his face calm but inward, as though he too had been quietly stirred by the *curandero's* words.

The *curandero* had touched a chord in me that vibrates still today.

*

Before we returned to the city, Emiliano took a detour. "I want to show you something," he said softly.

We drove off the main road, down a dusty path that opened into a small village. Time itself seemed to stretch and yawn in the warm air. Young Indigenous men lounged in hammocks strung between trees, their dark hair tied back, their shirts loose and open to the breeze. Some were smoking. All of them looked relaxed in a way that felt almost sacred, like they knew how to rest, not just physically, but in spirit.

They greeted us warmly, eyes curious and open. One asked where I lived, and when I told him America, several of them brightened.

"We plan to go there someday," one said, as though speaking of a distant star they fully intended to reach.

Then came the question: so unexpected, it felt like a gift.

"We heard that Americans landed on the moon and that when they got out of the spaceship, they walked in fields of high, tall grass, maize, and wheat. Is that true?"

Their faces held no irony but hope. Wonder.

I paused. I didn't want to let them down.

I smiled and said, "I didn't hear that. But it could be true."

They nodded, satisfied. Maybe they were humoring me, or perhaps they were wiser than I knew. Maybe, to them, the moon was not meant to be cold and empty but fertile with the dreams of Earth.

In their eyes, I saw something ancient. The belief that somewhere, somehow, what is beautiful and improbable might still be true.

Emiliano told me that they usually worked hard in the sun-soaked fields. But in the afternoon, they rested in hammocks, swaying gently in the shade like leaves in a breath of wind. They had nothing by American standards, but in that moment, I saw a kind of wealth we rarely understand: rest, community, imagination, the grace to believe in things not yet proven.

As we left the village, I carried their question with me. It felt like a parable, like something the *curandero* might have whispered.

*

Not long after settling into the rhythm of Mérida, I took two day-trips that left an indelible mark on my spirit. I traveled alone to Uxmal; on the other, I went with Heather to Chichén Itzá. Both ruins lay within reach of the city, yet they existed in dimensions far beyond time.

Uxmal felt like a revelation. There was a calm and majestic presence in how the ruins stood. The architecture was refined. The Great Pyramid emerged from the earth like a purposeful thought. I climbed the steps, feeling each stone, a note from an ancient hymn. From the top, the world looked softened by distance, bathed in golden light, and surrounded by silence of centuries past.

I thought of the pyramids of Egypt and the Roman temples I had once admired, but this was different. This was not the grandeur of empire or conquest. It was something more mysterious and organic. The buildings of Uxmal felt like they'd been grown, not built, as if the jungle itself had dreamed them into being.

A few days later, I stood before the Temple of Kukulkán, *El Castillo*, in Chichén Itzá. It struck me as another kind of power: geometrical, mathematical, symbolic. Ninety-one steps on each of four sides, totaling 364, and the summit platform is the 365th, a calendar carved in stone. At the equinox, the sun casts shadows that form the illusion of a serpent descending the pyramid. Quetzalcoatl, the Plumed Serpent, returning to the earth.

The site was expansive. The Temple of the Warriors loomed nearby, flanked by rows upon rows of carved stone columns, each bearing warriors adorned in feathers and headdresses. They stood like silent sentinels, guarding secrets I could only guess at.

Then there was the Great Ballcourt, the largest known in all of Mesoamerica. Its acoustics were uncanny, a whisper at one end carried with eerie clarity to the other.

But it was the Sacred Cenote that stirred me most. A great, round sinkhole, veiled in green and echoes, it had once received royal offerings, jewels, gold, human hearts. It was not a ruin. It was a portal.

With each site, I drew closer to the soul of a civilization that had charted the stars, built cities aligned with Venus, created hieroglyphic languages, and devised a number system based on the concept of zero long before it appeared elsewhere.

The Mayans had not merely built, they had understood.

*

Emiliano surprised me once more and took me to a place he didn't want to name.

We arrived at the base of a large hill covered with tangled greenery and ancient stone. There, carved into the side like the mouth of a forgotten god, was a vast cave. The entrance pulsated with energy.

Men were coming and going from it. All of them young, all Mexican, walking and talking to each other confidently. Some were drinking, others smoking with relaxed joy. Laughter floated in the air, and somewhere in the shadows, music played which seemed to come from everywhere all at once.

I followed Emiliano inside. The air was cool. The cave wasn't just a hollow space but a cathedral of earth. The walls rose around us, jagged and glistening. Stalactites hung like teeth, and the floor sloped gently downward, drawing us in.

There was no altar, no priest, no doctrine. And yet the place vibrated with the energy of ritual. The men weren't tourists. They weren't there to pray. But somehow, they were participating in something half-remembered, half-invented.

Brotherhood, maybe. Freedom. A gathering older than language.

No one looked twice at me. I was a stranger yet somehow not an intruder. I felt watched but not judged, observed but not unwelcome.

I leaned against the cool rock and let the music wash over me. This cave, this strange womb of stone and smoke, felt older than the ruins we had visited.

Someone shouted joyfully somewhere deep in the darkness. Bottles clinked. Someone danced, their silhouette flickering against the cavern wall like a spirit.

I turned to Emiliano and asked, "What is this place?"

He smiled. "A cave," he said. "But, also more." Emiliano turned to me with that familiar glint in his eye — half amusement, half secrecy — and almost whispered, "This is a place for men to disappear and reappear changed."

I looked around. The air inside the cave was thick not just with smoke or the scent of damp earth but with something like the residue of old stories. It didn't feel like a party. It felt older than that, as if the cave itself had memory. As if the laughter and music were just layers on top of something more profound.

"They come here," Emiliano continued, "to let go — to shed the skin they wear out there. No names, no burdens, no shame."

Women were there to welcome them. Many of them. They had their own reserved spaces carved in the outer parts of the cave covered with curtains.

I stared into the shadows. Some of the men were singing now, wordless melodies that echoed through the stone. There was joy but also measured reservation. It took me a few moments to realize that this was the strangest, most mystical brothel that probably existed in the whole world. I felt both drawn in by curiosity and repelled. I lingered at the edge, as if the cave was deciding how much of its secret I could carry.

"I've never seen anything like this," I murmured.

"You weren't meant to," he said. "Until now." And then he walked ahead, deeper into the cave.

She emerged from the dimness like a ghost. Tall, blonde, and striking, her presence was jarring in that sub-terranean world. She looked like a goddess. Her demeanor was calm but alert, and there was something almost theatrical in how she carried herself.

As she walked toward me, her expression changed, not seduction, not calculation, but something stranger. She looked at me with familiarity. She smiled as if I had returned to her after a long absence. Her voice was soft and affectionate when she spoke in Spanish, with an accent that suggested Castile or maybe Argentina.

There was nothing vulgar about her, yet something in her eyes betrayed a weariness she couldn't mask. The scent of other men lingered in the tired gentleness of her gestures and the practiced rhythm of her approach. She did not push herself on me. She merely offered.

But I was not tempted. Not out of judgment. Not out of moral superiority. But something in me recoiled, not from her but from the sadness of it all.

I didn't want to shame her. I didn't want to reject her, either. I pressed a folded bill into her hand. Her eyes met mine for a moment, searching. And in that moment, there was no client, no transaction, just two human beings in a cave carved into the bones of the Earth.

She just touched my arm lightly and vanished into one of the narrow chambers cut from rock.

I turned to Emiliano. He was watching me, unread-able. Maybe he had brought me there as a test, a lesson, or to show me one more shadow in a land thick with buried gods, hidden secrets, and forgotten truths.

We didn't speak as we walked back to the mouth of the cave. The air outside was calm and warm, the sky was starlit. I took a deep breath, reflecting on the mysterious place I had just visited and what I would carry with me.

Transition From Fieldwork to Research Fellowship

My time in the field had come to an end. I had to return to McGill University in Montreal to analyze the data I had gathered during my research. McGill offered me the opportunity to remain for an additional year to complete the analysis. Still, by then I had already applied for a fellowship in psychiatric research at Downstate Medical Center in Brooklyn, New York. I felt ready for a new challenge — one that would take me deeper into the evolving scientific understanding of mental illness.

Since the 1930s, striking differences had been noted between English and American psychiatrists in how they diagnosed affective disorders, particularly manic-depressive psychosis. British psychiatrists seemed to recognize these conditions far more frequently while their American counterparts tended to diagnose schizophrenia instead. In 1961,

Kramer conducted the first systematic review of this discrepancy. He found that schizophrenia was diagnosed about 50% less often in the U.K. than in the U.S., while manic-depressive psychosis was diagnosed almost nine times more often.

The questions raised by these findings were profound: Were the differences due to variations in psychiatric training? To distinct patient populations? Or were cultural attitudes toward emotional expression and eccentric behavior simply more tolerant in one society than the other? Whatever the reason, it was clear that diagnostic bias carried serious consequences. The treatment approaches diverged: American psychiatrists often prescribed antipsychotics while their British colleagues treated what they called "manic-depressive illness" with mood stabilizers such as lithium, and their patients tended to recover.

Around that time, I almost landed a position at Columbia University, assisting a British psychiatrist conducting a comparative study of psychiatric diagnoses in the U.K. and the U.S. His central thesis was that American psychiatrists were, to a large extent, blind to the existence of bipolar disorders — still known then as manic-depressive illness.

He invited me to his home for an interview and seemed eager to have me join his team. The study was to take place in the Bronx, and as a bilingual psychiatrist, I could have been instrumental in working with Spanish-speaking patients. Later, at a formal interview at Columbia, a few anthropologists asked whether I could communicate effectively with Puerto Rican participants in Spanish. I replied with an emphatic yes — which was entirely true — but for reasons still unclear to me, they didn't like my answer. Perhaps they felt I was unaware of the cultural nuances that distinguished Puerto Rican Spanish from Castilian. In any case, I wasn't hired.

I also applied to Harvard University's Department of Social Psychiatry, which was conducting fascinating research on the intersection of culture and mental health in French Canada. The director offered me a position in the training program, but before I could make arrangements, an administrator called to inform me that the grant funding had been exhausted. In hindsight, I could have gone to Boston anyway, found work at a hospital or a community mental health center, and attended the program independently. But at the time, I didn't realize that such an unconventional path was possible.

Ultimately, I accepted the fellowship in psychiatric research at Downstate Medical Center in Brooklyn, New York. It proved to be the right choice — an experience that would sharpen both my scientific curiosity and my awareness of how culture shapes the very way we define and treat mental illness.

Downstate Medical Center, Brooklyn, 1971

New York City wasn't mistreating me — far from it.

I liked the city, the pulse of it, the endless collisions of people and ideas, the sense that anything could happen. I loved wandering through the Upper East Side, where even the trees seemed to have manners, and ducking into a small French café after a long day at the hospital. The city's museums became my sanctuaries. The Metropolitan always had some dazzling new exhibit, Egyptian mummies one week, Japanese ink paintings the next. I would lose myself among the statues, sensing that art, like medicine, was another form of healing, only quieter.

At night, when I wasn't studying, I often slipped into the cheap seats of Broadway theaters or watched street performers in Washington Square. There was an energy in the air, raw, unfiltered, democratic. Everyone was from somewhere else; everyone was chasing something. It suited me perfectly.

Downstate Medical Center, in Brooklyn, was my daily laboratory, both literally and psychologically. I was enrolled in the Psychiatric Research Program, where I learned about the complex relationships between brain chemistry, behavior, and the human experience. I liked the rigor of it. Statistics, research design, and those monstrous hospital computers: machines that filled entire rooms and breathed cold air like prehistoric beasts.

To analyze my data from Jamaica on paternal absence, I learned to write primitive computer programs on stacks of punched cards. I'd carry my box of cards into the computer room like a priest bearing offerings. Minutes later, the printer would spit out long scrolls of results, cryptic hieroglyphs of numbers and symbols that felt like messages from another dimension. Sometimes they made sense; sometimes they didn't. But I loved the mystery of it, the feeling that I was on the frontier of something new.

To pay my rent, I worked part-time at an outpatient mental health center, where I made home visits with a nurse. The work could be unpredictable. Once, when we arrived at a patient's apartment, two policemen were already waiting, summoned by the patient himself. "Just making sure you are real doctors," he muttered from behind the chain lock. Another time, a woman insisted we remove our shoes and pray before we could administer her medication.

Some patients refused treatment outright; others accepted it reluctantly, convinced the injections were part of a government plot. Still, we persisted. With patience and gentle persuasion, we managed to get long-acting antipsychotics into arms that had once slammed doors in our faces. We learned to start with small doses to avoid side effects, always offering a prescription to ease any tremors or stiffness. The method worked. Slowly, impossibly, the unreachable became reachable.

Then came the curious experiment.

The director of the program, a brilliant, eccentric British psychiatrist with the air of an absent-minded philosopher, decided to train all the clinical staff in psycho-pharmacology. Everyone including social workers, therapists, and nurses. His idea was revolutionary: under his license, everyone could prescribe psychotropic drugs. It was intended to democratize psychiatry, freeing it from hierarchy.

"Psychiatry!" he declared in his clipped Oxford accent. "We should expand the number of prescribers not by hiring more MDs but by training the staff we have in psychopharmacology. We can make it easy for everyone to understand how to use these medications. We can save money and reach more patients."

It was bold. It was visionary. It was also, though we didn't know it yet, a disaster in the making.

Despite weeks of intensive training, most of the newly minted "prescribers" didn't know the difference between psychosis and depression, or how to choose the right medication for the right problem. Dosages went astray. Patients did not show improvement or experienced too many side effects. I began to see trouble brewing and reported my concerns to the director and a few senior psychiatrists.

He didn't take it well.

"Abad," he said, squinting at me over his glasses, "you are too conservative."

Maybe so. But soon after, he was promoted to oversee the entire New York State Mental Health System, and, astonishingly, tried the same grand experiment again on a larger scale. It didn't last long. Within months, the board caught wind of the chaos and promptly removed him. I never said, *I told you so,* but I confess the thought crossed my mind more than once.

For me, that chapter was closing. I had learned a great deal at Downstate, not only about brains and data but about the perilous beauty of human idealism.

By then, a quiet restlessness had returned, the familiar tug toward new horizons. I applied to Yale University, not expecting much. But life, like medicine, has a way of surprising us when we least expect it. One afternoon, a letter arrived.

"Congratulations," it said, "You've been accepted." The Department of Psychiatry at Yale was offering me a position with the Yale-Connecticut Community Mental Health Center in New Haven to be a part of a new program. The West Haven-Hill project. The Department had just received a grant to provide services to two underserved areas.

I put the letter down and stared at the window for a long time. Outside, the city lights shimmered on the East River. Somewhere in the distance, a siren wailed: a lonely, beautiful sound. I smiled, feeling that old surge of adventure again.

Another door had opened. Another path awaited. And so, I packed my bags, ready to see what lay beyond the next horizon. But first, I would spend my summer in Mallorca.

Mischief in Mallorca, 1972

I found myself in that delicious limbo between one life chapter and the next. I had just finished my psychiatric training research at Downstate Medical Center and accepted a job at Yale's Connecticut Mental Health Center. But before diving into the trenches of American Academia, I thought, *why not indulge in some European wellness?* The prescription? Sun, sea, and sensual possibility. The destination? Club Méditerranée, Mallorca edition. This was a place talked about in back alleys by backpackers in wine bars, rumored to be a den of international pleasure and endless buffet lines.

I had visions of sultry evenings of flamenco and laughter, moonlit swims, spontaneous love affairs with mysterious women. A paradise of fresh seafood, chilled rosé, and tanned bodies unburdened by time or responsibility.

Marketing, as usual, had done its job. The reality was less Riviera and more rigid itinerary.

I arrived full of hope and hormones, only to find myself locked out of all the good stuff. You had to reserve your fun in advance like a dentist appointment. The sailing slots were booked solid, the Moroccan restaurant was full for the week, and by the time I got to the stables, the horses were already trotting. The myth of Club Med promised hedonism; what I got was a cruise ship on land.

Still, I gave it my best. I played beach volleyball, drank sangria alone at sunset, and tried not to look too pitiful on the dance floor. At night, I walked along the beach pretending I was in a Godard film, *l'homme solitaire,* the intellectual rogue on a Mediterranean quest for something vaguely existential.

One day, with the taste of sea salt and Chanel No. 5 of some French women lingering, I rented a car and drove across the island. Palma de Mallorca unfolded like a dreamscape of orange groves, olive trees, and blue waves crashing against limestone cliffs. I wandered through sleepy fishing villages, where men played dominos, smoked, and drank coffee in the outdoor cafes of vibrant plazas, women were absent, and cats outnumbered people. Finally, I arrived at the Caves of Drach, which was a true marvel.

There were stalagmites dripping from cathedral-high ceilings, a subterranean lake shimmering like spilled moonlight, and gondoliers in tuxedos gliding silently through darkness while classical music echoed through the stone belly of the earth.

It was like stepping into the womb of the planet. The sight was both breathtaking and surreal. I still felt incredibly lonely. Even surrounded by beauty, good food, and flirtation, I felt an ache.

There was a missing piece in my life, a woman. There was a soul-shaped hole. I left Mallorca sunburned, kissed, lonely, and still searching. But I had a story, and sometimes that's enough to maintain the heart's rhythm.

A Wedding in Maryland, 1973

It was a long drive, the kind that stretches more in the soul than on the map. Boston faded into the background for me and my girlfriend at the time. I had met Lynn in Spain while she was vacationing in Madrid with a girlfriend. Now, one of her high school girlfriends was getting married, and she asked me to escort her to the wedding. Maryland loomed ahead like an unwritten story waiting to be shared. I was bringing Lynn home. Not to mine, but to hers. There was weight in that. Not heavy, just significant.

She rode beside me, legs tucked up, hair loose in the wind, humming to a song that wasn't playing. I thought, *this is what trust looks like.* Not in declarations or grand gestures but a woman barefoot, soft-eyed, letting me steer her back to the place that made her.

We arrived after dark, the house glowing like a lighthouse through the trees. Fireflies stitched the dusk, porch lights hummed, and she bounded up the steps with a laugh that broke the silence. I followed more slowly, aware I wasn't just entering a house; I was entering her history.

That night, under a slanted ceiling in a small upstairs room, I lay awake listening to the creaks and sighs of someone else's home. Morning came with a whisper and a warning.

"Vincent, we have a problem." Her father, she explained, had heard I was Spanish. And to him, that meant shame.

"Should I leave?" I asked.

Lynn shook her head. "No, once he sees you, it'll be fine." She didn't say the rest: that my pale skin and blue eyes would spare me his prejudice. The thought stung, but I understood.

Downstairs, her mother greeted me with warmth and cinnamon-toast hugs, relief written across her face when she saw I looked like "one of them." She fed me eggs and grits and, I suspected, went straight to negotiate with her husband.

When her father appeared, it was with quiet gravity. His handshake was firm, his tone measured. Not welcoming, not hostile, but with the tone of a man deciding whether I belonged. He didn't embrace me, but allowed me into his plans, his car, and his order of things. That was his way of acceptance.

The wedding itself unfolded with small-town grace: a caravan of cars, casseroles, laughter, a church that smelled of wood and wildflowers. At the reception, I braced for suspicion, but it never came. People smiled, made space at their tables, and passed me platters as though I'd always been there. Even her father softened his disapproval into something more like uneasy respect. But it wasn't the vows or the celebration that stayed with me. It was what came after.

The next day, Lynn had something else in mind.

She guided me down to the coast, away from the small towns, wedding energy, and the polite architecture of other people's lives. We drove until the roads gave way to dunes, and the wind began to smell salty. We arrived at Assateague Island National Seashore.

I had never heard of it before. It was a long, narrow island with thirty-seven miles of wild Atlantic coast straddling Maryland and Virginia.

"A national reserve," she told me, "is protected land. Sacred, in its own way."

At first, the usual beauty struck me: the stretch of sand like a ribbon pulled loose from the continent, the slow breathing of the ocean, the wind weaving through the salt marshes and maritime forests. It was the kind of landscape that clears the mind and makes the soul sit up straighter.

Then, there appeared the horses — real, living horses. Untethered, trotting along the beach like they owned it, which in a way, they did. Part white, part brown, their coats looked like abstract paintings. They moved with that unhurried confidence of creatures that had never fenced in. Wild mustangs. The entire island felt mythical. Lynn smiled as I stared.

"They're descendants of Spanish horses," she said. "Conquistadors. Some of their ships wrecked off the coast centuries ago. The horses swam to shore. Not only did they survive but they thrived. They made this place theirs."

I didn't speak for a while.

The image hit me somewhere deep. The idea of those animals thrown from the wreckage of empire, washed ashore into an alien wilderness, bones shaking, lungs burning, yet choosing to endure and claim the beach as their own.

There was something in that story I needed to hear. Something about broken beginnings and accidental arrivals. About surviving when you weren't expected to. About how wildness doesn't have to be tamed to be beautiful.

I stood there watching them, hooves in the surf, manes tangled with salt and wind, and thought: *This is what freedom looks like*. It means to belong nowhere and yet be entirely at home.

Lynn reached for my hand. We stood silently as the mustangs moved farther down the shoreline. A living memory of something resilient and raw was taking form within me.

The Spanish Clinic and Psychoanalysis at Yale University, 1972–78

When I left Spain, I carried two dreams in the same suitcase.

One was academic. I wanted to teach, publish, and do research that mattered.

The other was personal. I wanted to belong in a place where the mind could breathe intellectually.

In 1972, I arrived at Yale. For a young immigrant doctor, the name felt like a seal of approval. I told myself I had reached the mountain. I also told myself a story I wanted to believe: that talent and effort would be enough.

Yale was not an Olympus. It was a working institution with rules, hierarchies, and blind spots. I learned that slowly and the hard way, like most useful lessons.

My job was clear. I provided psychiatric care to the Hill neighborhood in New Haven. The streets were rough. Many houses were boarded up. The sidewalks were broken. Poverty was not an idea there. It was the air people breathed. And yet Puerto Rican flags hung from porches. Bright color against gray. Families carried pride, grief, humor, faith, and stubborn hope at the same time.

I also supervised residents and lectured on cross-cultural psychiatry. I carried a chronic schizophrenia caseload. Two nurses worked with me who were tireless and deeply kind. Across town, a Black psychiatrist was assigned to West Haven. The logic was simple and blunt: a Black doctor and a Brown one — because it was assumed a Spaniard was not white — were assigned to minority patients.

At first, I felt grateful. I was an immigrant. I had a job at Yale. I could support myself. I could learn.

Then I began to understand the dominant culture of the place. Psychoanalysis was not just one approach. It was the doctrine. Freud was the prophet. The faculty were the high priests. To call yourself "eclectic," as I did, was a kind of heresy.

Some of my residents treated young WASP women with polished anxiety. They were articulate and introspective. They could talk intelligently for hours. They were considered "ideal patients." They moved them from one trainee to the next, year after year, like a baton passed down a hallway. There was nothing wrong with helping them for years. The problem was what happened to everyone else.

That is where my other education began.

Latino patients began arriving at the mental health center. They came quietly. Many were ashamed. Many were desperate. They were often misunderstood from the first sentence. They did not speak the language well. Even when they did, they did not speak the culture. Their suffering had its own grammar: faith, family duty, spirits, guilt, shame, migration, poverty, and the long memory of humiliation and trauma.

I was the only bilingual clinician there, so they were sent to me.

At first, I thought the problem was translation. I was wrong. They did not need a dictionary. They needed a place where their reality would not be mocked, minimized, or diagnosed as superstition.

That was when I proposed the Spanish Clinic. Not a clinic where we simply spoke Spanish. A bilingual and bi-cultural clinic. A place where patients could tell the truth in their own words and not be punished for it. A place where a Puerto Rican mother could talk about a curse, a saint, or a spirit and not be labeled irrational before anyone asked what the belief meant to her life.

Not everyone liked the idea. In a staff meeting, a senior professor walked in red with anger. "This will only reinforce the superstitions of these people!" he shouted.

I remember staying calm. I did not want a fight. I wanted a clinic. "We are not here to promote superstition," I said. "We are here to understand cultural and spiritual lives and treat people with that understanding."

Part of my confidence came from talking with and befriending a Yale anthropologist who studied Puerto Rican *curanderismo* with respect. She understood why community healers were trusted. They spoke the patient's language. They carried the community's authority to heal. They did not treat people as cases but as family.

I also learned at McGill and from E. Fuller Torrey that healers and healing are always shaped by culture. The form changes, but the human need does not. Empathy can ease suffering even before the first pill is swallowed. That does not mean every belief is helpful. Some beliefs can trap people in fear. Some "healers" can do harm. But feeling unwelcome and labeled as ignorant or superstitious is also harmful. You can listen to a strange belief without humiliating the person who holds it.

So we built the clinic. We used medication. We used problem-solving therapy. We used common sense. We used humility. In that setting, traditional psychoanalysis often felt like asking someone to read Kafka in Latin while their rent was overdue and their child was sick. The results surprised people. They should not have, but they did.

Patients improved for many reasons. Medication helped. I found a combination of medications that worked like magic with problems like anger and irritability. Practical problem-solving therapy helped. But something else helped too: being seen. Trust itself became a kind of medicine. When people feel safe, they tell the truth. When they tell the truth, you can finally help them.

One afternoon, a *curandera* came to meet me. She sat in my office and shared stories from her own childhood, including traumas. We were not enemies. We became friendly. We were two humans trying to reduce suffering, each shaped by a different tradition. I remember thinking: *why build walls when trust is possible?*

Word spread. On Saturday mornings, community leaders came to my apartment. We drank *cafecito*. They talked about burdens and marital problems they had never said out loud. It was not a seminar. It was not a theory. It was a human life, sitting on a chair, telling the truth to another person. No appointments, no fees. Just human sharing.

At the clinic, I worked closely with two social workers who taught me a great deal. Juan Ramos, who was Puerto Rican, helped me understand the texture of Puerto Rican life — its humor, pride, spiritual practices, and wounds. He helped me see what outsiders often miss. Not the "exotic" parts, but the daily reality. Elizabeth Boyd — Lily, as I called her — was American, steady, and sharp. She was also an incredible cook, which is not irrelevant. Food is a language of care. Lily helped me write clinical papers. She worked with me on a National Institute of Mental Health grant to provide alcoholism services in New Haven.

We got the funding and suddenly, I had staff, resources, and a certain kind of attention. People noticed me. I told myself again: I have arrived. But the old desire did not go away. I still wanted to do research. I still wanted mentorship. I still wanted the kind of academic growth I had imagined when I left Spain.

I tried to join a research team studying violence in a Connecticut prison. A British psychiatrist was testing whether lithium reduced violent behavior compared with placebo. The work mattered. He was willing to include me. But I did not receive support from the leadership of the community mental health center. The doors did not open. I felt blocked. I felt, again, like an outsider who had done the work but was not invited into the inner rooms.

That is where my feelings got complicated, and through the years, I tried to stay honest about it. It would be easy to write myself as the victim in that story and sometimes I did. How I've thought about it seems to always change shape to fit the mood of the moment. But time teaches you that memory is not a courtroom transcript. It is a narrative we can keep revising to survive.

Yale did give me something. It gave me real patients. It gave me a chance to build something useful that had not been done before. It gave me colleagues who worked hard with me. And it also showed me its limits. Part of those limits was linked to psychoanalysis.

I was first introduced to and allured by psychoanalysis long before Yale. I was a medical student when it placed its elegant hook in my imagination. Psychiatry felt too simple then. Psychotic or neurotic. Crazy or miserable. It seemed like a cheap map of a vast country.

Then I met the only psychoanalyst in town, Dr. Pertejo. She had sharp eyes. You felt examined before you spoke. A group of us gathered in her office like disciples. We read Freud with the seriousness of monks. Dreams, slips of the tongue, childhood scenes — everything had a hidden meaning. We wanted depth. We wanted the secret chamber beneath the basement.

Down the hall, the neurologists rolled their eyes. They had EEGs and spinal taps. They had the confidence of people who can point to something on a scan. To them, we were poets with stethoscopes. To us, they were electricians who never asked about the person at the end of the wire.

For a while, psychoanalysis felt intoxicating. It made suffering feel meaningful. It turned pain into a story. It made you feel like an intellectual. If you wanted to sound profound, Freud was your man.

Then reality began to interrupt my devotion in small, almost comic ways.

I owned a green wool jacket with suede elbow patches. The perfect costume for a young Freudian. I never wore it. I started analyzing myself. *What was I afraid of? Envy? Exposure? Father issues? Mother issues? A childhood trauma involving a dog? Why was it that I had not worn that jacket, not even once, when I bought it with some enthusiasm, thinking it made me look like a real university professor?*

Months later, I finally put it on, and my arms started burning. The wool was unbearably itchy. The problem was not unconscious. It was dermatological. I was allergic to the material.

That jacket did more to cure my Freudian fever than a semester of seminars. I always thought that psychoanalysis was not appropriate for everyday, regular clinical practice. Psychoanalysis was slow and expensive. Many patients received little relief while their lives collapsed outside the office for decades. But inefficiency was not the real problem. Harm was.

For decades, many analysts blamed autism on "refrigerator mothers," as if maternal coldness caused the condition. They blamed schizophrenia on the "schizophrenogenic mother," a phrase so cruel it should have been rejected on moral grounds alone. I sat through seminars where these ideas were presented with certainty. Families suffered. Mothers wept. And the analysts kept interpreting.

In the 1970s, I witnessed how fiercely psychoanalysts defended their field and the arrogant contempt they held for anyone who didn't share their ideology. I remember a psychologist at the Yale Institute telling me that psychoanalysts might treat only a few patients, while at the Mental Health Center, where we saw many more patients, treated no one.

Another example of this arrogance was in the case of Dr. Osheroff, a kidney specialist who fell into severe depression. He was admitted to Chestnut Lodge, a famous psychoanalytic hospital. He begged for medication. His family begged. Instead, he was given more talk, more interpretation, more talk therapy. He deteriorated badly. He finally left the hospital against medical advice, received antidepressants elsewhere, and quickly recovered. He sued Chestnut Lodge. The case forced psychoanalysts to confront their own illusions.

At around the same time, places like Camarillo Hospital in California were treating schizophrenia with a blend of medication and psychotherapy. Many psychoanalysts thought at the time that even schizophrenia could be treated with psychoanalysis. Patients improved with medication alone, but even more so when a person showed interest in them, and therapy was added. Later, I read Frederick Crews and E. Fuller Torrey. Crews stripped away the myth of Freud the scientist and showed the power of Freud the storyteller. Torrey argued that psychoanalysis had pulled psychiatry away from serious mental illness for far too long, while patients paid the cost.

That did not mean psychoanalysis was worthless. It can comfort people who resonate with a relevant story and offer a sense of meaning. Meaning matters. But meaning is not always medicine. When people are suffering badly, comfort and handholding are not enough.

The Spanish Clinic helped settle this argument inside me.

It taught me that people do not come to us as theories. They come as people who live lives with problems, sometimes physical, sometimes psychological, sometimes relational, and sometimes you just don't know and you have to be open-minded enough not to rush to produce an instant answer. They want to sleep. They want to stop shaking. They want to work. They want to stop fighting at home. They want to feel human again. And above all, they want to feel valued, that they matter. If we can help them with an effective medication plan, practical therapy, and genuine respect, we should do so. We should not force them to believe a fabricated story.

When I look back, I feel proud of the Spanish Clinic. Not in a heroic way. In a simple way. We built a place that reduced suffering for people who had been invisible. The clinic demonstrated that psychiatry can be both scientific and culturally respectful. It can honor tradition without surrendering to superstition. It can educate without humiliating. It can treat someone without erasing the person.

And still, I also remember the restlessness I carried. The sense that I was helping Yale more than Yale was helping me. I was not being mentored. I was not growing as I wanted. I had done something useful, and I also felt stalled.

In time, I left. I joined Hartford Hospital and the University of Connecticut. I met the woman who would become my wife. My life became richer and more grounded. I learned to live and work among real people and real patients, who taught me more than any theory could.

I carry one regret. I wish I had asked Juan Ramos and Lily to continue the work after I left. I hope they knew what they helped build and that they mattered.

If I could do it again, I think I would do a few things differently. I would bring more American-born clinicians into the clinic early, so the cultural bridge would have been in place. I might have even put *café con leche* in the waiting room and displayed cultural decorations as a sign: you are welcome here.

What I know for sure is this.

Psychoanalysis taught me the seduction of hidden meanings. It taught me how easily we can mistake elegance and understanding for truth. It taught me that intelligent and sophisticated individuals, when relying on ideologies, can harm others while believing they are helping. Psychoanalysis is an ideology similar to religion in many ways. Both offer satisfying explanations that appear to provide meaningful understanding of a complex world, yet shun a scientific or evidence-based approach. They both can help when administered with compassion.

The Spanish Clinic taught me something important. People heal faster when they feel seen and their beliefs are valued. "Being seen" and "being valued" are not metaphors. They're essential to human beings.

How I Met My Beautiful Wife

There are moments in life when destiny shifts almost unnoticed until one day you look back and realize that everything started with a single, luminous encounter. When I left Yale and began my new life at Hartford Hospital, I believed I had finally found peace. I managed an outpatient clinic, cared for my private patients, and returned each evening to my beautiful condo on the Connecticut shoreline, overlooking the North Shore of Long Island.

From my bedroom window, the world unfolded like a living poem. Birds glided over the marshlands. The seasons moved with a precision that humbled me: green turned to gold, gold to rust, leaves tumbling from branches like tiny prayers returning to the earth. It was paradise, but a solitary one. Beauty surrounded me, but it could not fill the empty place beside me. Something essential was missing: a companion, a partner, a woman to share the quiet joys and more profound mysteries of life. I thought back to my time in Yucatán and the *cuarandero's* comment. *When would I find the woman who would walk beside me? The one who would know me better than I knew myself?*

Then fate intervened.

One day, the Mayor of New Britain invited all bilingual Hispanic physicians to a luncheon in our honor. I went expecting nothing more than polite speeches and hand-shakes. Instead, I stepped into a moment that would change my life. There she was sitting with her parents at a table next to a Cuban doctor I happened to know. From the moment we spoke, the atmosphere between us shifted, as if the whole room had tilted slightly toward our conversation.

She told me she was a surgical resident at New Britain General Hospital. Her focus, determination, and eyes that showed both strength and kindness drew me in instantly. I asked for her phone number, and she cleverly gave me the number to an auto garage to test the level of my interest. Perhaps she expected our connection would end there. But destiny is stubborn, and so was I. In my pursuit to know her more, I went to her work.

When we finally had our first date, our conversation picked up as if it had just paused. Something unusual was beginning to happen, something neither of us could ignore: a connection. We had many things in common.

Only a few months later, in New Haven, Connecticut, we got married. First, we went to the town's clerk office, and a few days later we had a whole wedding at the most prominent Catholic church in New Haven. She was Catholic and I was a recovering Catholic. It was a quick decision, but when the heart finds its match, time becomes meaningless. You know. She was the woman I had been searching for and waiting for through years of exile, study, heartbreak, and wandering. She was the missing element in my journey, the luminous light I had been steadily pursuing without even knowing her name.

For our honeymoon, we planned to escape the disciplined routine of our lives to Bermuda. We were two young physicians stepping into the unknown together, carrying nothing but hope, purpose, and love.

The Bermuda Triangle, 1979

When the honeymoon was over, I was grateful above all that my wife was alive, and I hadn't killed her.

Let me explain.

It's not that I planned to murder or harm her in any way. Quite the opposite as I was trying to impress her. You know, do the things that make a woman say, "Wow, I picked a winner." But somewhere between the boat rental desk and the middle of the Bermuda Triangle, things got complicated.

One sunny afternoon, I rented a small motorboat to take my bride for a ride across a shimmering, vast Atlantic Ocean. She wanted to drive, and I, in the name of love, handed over the controls like a gentleman. That's when I discovered I'd married a speed demon.

She hit the throttle with the enthusiasm of a NASCAR rookie, and the boat began to slap the waves with the force of a jackhammer. Up and down we went with water flying everywhere and my kidneys rattling like dice in a cup. She whooped with joy. I clutched the seat and prayed.

I thought, *She's brave. She's wild. I married a storm in a sundress.*

The next day, still recovering from whiplash and wounded masculinity, we walked by the pier and noticed several charming little sailboats rocking gently in the breeze. Romantic. Peaceful. This is exactly my kind of boat. But I thought they came with a sailor. I envisioned us lounging, hand in hand, while a friendly Bermudian captain did all the work and pointed out seabirds.

Then came the fatal question.

"Can you sail?" the man asked.

Now, I had sailed a Sunfish once or twice in college (if by sail you mean mostly drift and occasionally panic), but pride is mighty, so I squared my shoulders and said, "Yes."

Ten minutes later, I was on a sailboat, handling it alone. My beautiful new wife watched me expectantly, as though I might gracefully part the waters like Moses with a mast.

At first, it went surprisingly well. I caught the gentle wind in the sail, adjusted the rudder, and we were off. I began to relax, and even enjoyed myself. My wife smiled at me, clearly impressed. I thought, *I can do this. I am competent. I am the man.*

Fifteen minutes later or so, things changed. The situation took a sudden and dramatic turn for the worse.

The breeze turned into a gale. Dark clouds rolled in with suspicious urgency. Waves began slapping the hull with the enthusiasm I'd hoped to avoid since yesterday. Like a gunshot, the sail snapped, causing it to flail rapidly, wildly, and out of control. The boat tilted. It was close to capsizing. We had entered the Bermuda Triangle. Still smiling faintly, my wife asked, "Is it supposed to do that?"

"No," I said, gripping the tiller with both hands, trying to remember anything from that one summer sailing class I mostly skipped.

Worriedly, she confessed, "I have to tell you something."

"What?" I asked, not sure I wanted to know.

"I can't swim."

That stopped me cold.

The wind didn't stop. The waves didn't stop. But something inside me did. I turned to look at her, this woman who had practically tried to launch us into orbit in a motorboat the day before, now calmly sitting on a wind-tossed sailboat revealing that if we tipped over, she'd sink like an anchor.

"You're telling me this now?" I said, in that slightly high-pitched voice men use when fear and marital diplomacy collide.

"I didn't think it would matter," she said.

"Well, it matters now!"

I tightened my grip on the tiller, adjusted the sail with the panic of someone trying to land a plane without training and a very calm co-pilot who just admitted she can't survive a crash.

That was the moment my internal monologue became entirely prayer based. *God, I know I just got married, but if you could help me not drown my wife today, I'd be very grateful.*

The wind howled. The boat leaned hard to one side. She grabbed the rail. Her long hair whipped across her face, and I still remember thinking in the madness of it all: *This is not how I imagined our honeymoon ending.* In some alternate timeline, I would be giving a tragic interview: "Yes, officer, she was a wonderful woman. I should never have lied to the boatman." I also thought, *if she dies, her father will come after me, and I will be a dead man.*

Somehow, I got us back to shore by pure luck and terror. I was drenched, and she was giddy. The boat was intact, though my ego was not.

That evening, we eventually laughed about it over rum drinks and sunburns. I realized something I'd carry far beyond Bermuda: marriage is not about looking impressive. It's about keeping the boat upright when the weather turns. It's about telling the truth, even when your pride wants to show off. And sometimes, it's about surviving your good intentions.

Love, I learned, isn't measured in smooth sailing. It's measured in whether you can make it back to shore and still laugh about it later.

My First Computer, 1984

On January 24, 1984, the Macintosh was introduced with a powerful Super Bowl commercial that made it feel less like a product launch and more like a revolution for humanity. Apple promised something groundbreaking: a computer so simple your grandmother could use it. That was exactly the computer I needed.

At the time, I was living in Manhasset, New York, watching IBM dominate the world with its intimidating machines. Every time I entered an IBM store, the clerks spoke a language somewhere between ancient Greek and Martian engineering. They answered questions I didn't ask and ignored the ones I did. Their computers felt like medical devices with no instruction manual.

Then came the Mac.

An Apple store finally opened in Manhasset after months of anticipation. I walked in like a pilgrim entering a sacred site. There it was: the small beige box that promised salvation. It was modern. Friendly. It seemed to smile at you when you turned it on.

It was expensive — painfully so, especially with the printer — but I didn't hesitate. I bought one immediately and strutted out of that store like someone carrying the future under their arm.

The Macintosh had 128K of RAM. Yes, kilobytes. Today, your refrigerator has more memory. But back then, it didn't matter. It was everything Apple claimed — simple, elegant, and remarkably easy to use. No instruction manuals thicker than medical textbooks and no cold, cryptic commands. You plugged it in, and *voila*, you could start writing. It just worked.

It came with software for writing and drawing. The printer connected smoothly, without tears or curses. Within minutes, I was printing letters that looked more polished than anything I'd ever typed on my bulky typewriter. And once I created a template, I could print a dozen versions, changing only a name or an address. This was the real purpose for this new machine. Let me explain.

At the time, my wife — a brilliant, fierce, and young surgeon — was completing her residency in General Surgery at North Shore University Hospital, part of Cornell. She lived and breathed surgery. Attending surgeons practically fought for the chance to have her scrub in with them. She was that talented.

But there was one obstacle: she wanted to specialize in plastic surgery, and in 1984, women were about as welcome in that field as polar bears in Miami. They doubted women's hands, stamina, commitment, and especially their ability to avoid getting pregnant at inconvenient times. It was prejudice disguised as concern.

But I knew her talent. I had seen her hands. I had watched her discipline. She just needed an opportunity, and I had 128 kilobytes of revolutionary power.

I headed to the medical library and found a directory listing every plastic surgery residency program in the country. All 103 of them. One afternoon, fueled by hope and excitement about new technology, I sat at that Macintosh and wrote a personalized letter to each program director. One hundred and three letters, each printed perfectly on our brand-new Apple printer. It took me only an hour to print them all. And then we mailed them.

We waited. Weeks went by. Silence. The kind of silence that makes you rethink your choices. Then, one day, three envelopes arrived. Not thirty. Not thirteen. Just three. But three was enough.

One was from the University of Illinois at Chicago. They wanted her letters of recommendation. When those letters arrived, packed with praise for her surgical skills, discipline, and character, they couldn't refuse her. They offered her a spot.

From there, her world expanded. She trained with top plastic surgeons in New York, Miami, and on the West Coast. Today, she is a respected and successful plastic surgeon in Boca Raton, known for her artistry in facial rejuvenation and facelifts.

That Macintosh 128K had the memory of a goldfish, but it changed our lives forever. It wasn't just a computer. It was a tool of possibility. A doorway. A small beige box that helped turn our destiny around.

Chicago, 1984-1991

Mobility, in the American context, is both a privilege and a price to pay. The freedom to pursue better jobs or advanced training fuels the nation's ingenuity, but it also demands that families uproot themselves and plant new roots in unfamiliar soil, starting again — which we did.

We moved for my wife's career after her acceptance into one of the most competitive plastic surgery residency programs in the country at the University of Illinois in Chicago. I admired her ability to chase challenging goals with a kind of quiet intensity, and I was willing to follow.

I, too, found my place. I joined the Illinois State Psychiatric Institute, the crown jewel of the state's psychiatric research hospital system. It was the kind of institution where you didn't just treat illness, you studied it, questioned it, and debated it in conference rooms where reputations were made and unmade by the force of a single idea. I was given charge of

11 East, an inpatient psychiatric unit with a defined catchment area in greater Chicago. My fluency in Spanish and bicultural background became valuable assets particularly in serving the city's large Mexican American population.

The Director of the Institute, a sharp, perceptive man, seemed to recognize something in me early on, a particular clarity of purpose. We developed an excellent rapport, as with the Clinical Director. These relationships, I quickly learned, are not just administrative conveniences; they shape the atmosphere around you. In every institution, there is an invisible current of perception; how those in power see you shapes how others respond to you. People notice, even without saying so.

Never underestimate the power of being trusted by those who hold the keys. There are entire books written about it. *How to Win Friends and Influence People* remains a classic. The essence is simple: be curious, not combative; find common ground; speak less and observe more; and above all, be useful.

My wife, always the scientist, was not content to learn technical skills in surgery. She started her own research project by interviewing breast cancer patients in hospital wards across the city. She had a suspicion that women who often used talc powder and deodorants might face a higher risk. Her interviews were thorough, and her statistical analyses were detailed and comprehensive. Ultimately, her suspicion was confirmed: a strong, statistically significant correlation was discovered. She also identified notable links between red meat consumption and smoking to increased breast cancer risk.

The paper was never published, and I still feel angry about that. Perhaps it was ahead of its time because years later, the link between talc and cancer finally made headlines. She saw it earlier but was never recognized.

Not all my work in Chicago was framed by research and professional ease. One patient left a lasting mark on me.

He was a young man whose psychiatric presentation changed from one admission to the next. At times, he was floridly psychotic, paranoid, withdrawn, and unreachable. At other times, he swung toward mania, becoming charismatic and grandiose. We diagnosed him with schizoaffective disorder and began treatment. He was prescribed Thioridazine, a common antipsychotic at the time.

Then, something shifted. His posture grew twisted. His muscles jerked involuntarily. His eyes seemed to pull in directions beyond his control. He had developed tardive dystonia, a rare and cruel side effect. I felt a deep responsibility. After all, I had prescribed the medication that caused it.

I took him to see several neurologists. Their diagnosis confirmed what I already feared. Treatments were proposed, tried, and failed. Then, almost by accident, we discovered something remarkable. He responded to Verapamil, a calcium channel blocker. His symptoms eased, nearly as if a switch had been turned off. The real dilemma remained: how to manage his psychosis without triggering the movement disorder again.

Dr. Ovsiev, a neurologist at the University of Chicago, both kind and inquisitive, became interested in the case. He arranged for the patient to be admitted to his unit for further study. We ultimately published a joint case report in the British Journal of Psychiatry. It was a small victory, but it mattered. For the patient. For us. For the field.

Chicago experienced its seasons, both meteorologically and metaphorically. Winters were so cold that running out of gas could be deadly; you might freeze in your car if you were unlucky enough to be stranded in the middle of nowhere. Spring and summer, however, were pleasant. There was a park near our house where, every summer, a local theater group would build a makeshift stage and perform Shakespeare. We would walk there on warm evenings, carrying folding chairs, a thermos of coffee between us, and sit under the stars listening to Hamlet or Twelfth Night. Those evenings, with their poetic rhythms and Midwestern twilight, reminded us that medicine and science are not separate from art. They all reach for the same mysterious pulse beneath the surface of things.

My wife finished her residency with honors, but she aspired to something more advanced: cosmetic surgery. Florida offered chances, and the sunlit coasts called to us like an echo of a different kind of life.

So, once again, we packed up. Uprooted. Began again.

We learned that, too, is part of the American story.

Florida, 1991-present

After Chicago, we let the road tilt south, following a sun that seemed to promise both clarity and reinvention. My wife found her place in Boca Raton, opening her plastic surgery practice in a strip of town where palms leaned into the heat and storefront awnings faded over time from the salty air. I began at the South County Community Health Center, its hallways echoing with the murmur of two languages blending in the waiting room.

Boca, in those years, was a wealthy town moving at a slow pace. Summers arrived like a held breath where streets emptied, lawns baked in stillness, and even the ocean seemed quiet. The air smelled of hibiscus, and in the late afternoons, heat shimmered over asphalt as if the whole place were a mirage. People waved from across the street, their smiles wide, their politeness deliberate. But sometimes, the calm surface broke. A colleague's first words to my Cuban-born wife were, "This is not a good place for you. Why don't you try Miami?"

The words hung heavy in the humid air, like truth hiding in the wrong tone.

Florida's restlessness has always been there. Spain once claimed this land, then relinquished it in 1819, trading it to the United States for $5 million and a relinquished claim to Texas. I carried that history with me when I took my young son to St. Augustine. We walked the ramparts of the Castillo de San Marcos, the *coquina* walls cool under our palms, their rough surfaces smelling faintly of the sea from which they had risen. Those walls had absorbed cannon fire and centuries of siege yet still stood.

My son was spellbound. Back home, he built a model of the fort for school and won first prize. I remember the sound of his laughter when he brought the ribbon to me; it was a kind of music I have kept.

Boca has its own origin stories. Addison Mizner once saw it as a Mediterranean paradise which shows in the grand hotel he built, where I sometimes attended medical meetings. Certain arches and tiles felt like stolen pieces of Seville or Granada. During the war, those same hallways served as hospital wards and later, the land where Florida Atlantic University now stands was a secret radar research site. This place quietly bears its reinventions, as if each past life still lingers in the shade of the royal palms.

My wife earned her privileges at Boca Raton Community Hospital, a place born out of a mother's grief, after her two children died in a town lacking emergency care. In the ER, she worked through long nights under the harsh white glare of surgical lamps, her voice steady even when the room was not.

From the South County Community Mental Health Center, I moved to the Veterans Administration, initially managing the outpatient clinic in West Palm Beach, then commuting to Miami for over twenty years. The VA air always carried something challenging to define. Something like an underlying sense of service and pride from anyone associated with it. There, I met men and women who had experienced war and had been hardened by battles. Normandy's beaches, Korea's icy hills, Vietnam's jungles, Iraq's deserts, Afghanistan's mountains. Some bore their scars openly while others carried them so deep, they could only be seen through an averted gaze. Their patriotism remained strong, even when their stories spoke of betrayal. Others had moral injuries and felt guilty for what they had done. Sometimes, those things were so hard and painful to describe that the VA has an alternative system of clinics, Vet Centers, where sensitive records of their conversations and therapy sessions are not kept.

Once, in a circle of Vietnam veterans, we mapped the war using real military maps and memories: U.S. bases surrounded by Vietcong, villages divided in their loyalty for survival, and a government in Saigon speaking for only a fraction of its people. We discussed terrain and how a land that is home can also be a weapon. None of us said it outright, but there was a truth in the air: you cannot occupy what you do not understand, and the war could not be won, despite the military might of the U.S.

I was honored to serve as the Medical Director of a day rehab program for veterans battling substance abuse. It was highly successful but not because of me. The staff was highly dedicated; they really loved their patients, and the patients loved them back. They provided the veterans with the much-needed support and TLC, but also everyone understood how difficult it is to treat individuals caught in the grip of substance addiction, as they often relapse and stop attending treatment.

Our patients showed up every day without fail. We had a secret method, not just the therapy, but also food. Two hot square meals a day were brought directly from the hospital kitchen, courtesy of the U.S. Government. The smell of baked bread, nourishing meals, and the warmth of coffee cups in their hands seemed to soften something inside them. I realized that free nourishment feeds and heals more than just the body.

When I retired from the VA, I thought my clinical journey had come to an end. But the Caridad Center, an unlikely refuge of compassion for the uninsured, drew me in with four hundred retired doctors, a whole dental team, and a waiting room that always overflowed. There, I met a little girl, her shoulders trembling as she cried because her teacher told her she could be deported.

It was in those rooms that representatives from the FAU Christine E. Lynn College of Nursing found me. Their invitation led to my work at the Florida Atlantic University Northwest Community Health Alliance (FAU/NCHA) Community Health Center, and the Louis and Anne Green Memory and Wellness Center where we studied the wide range of ways cognitive impairment presents itself in the elderly as well as psychiatric complications, and the profound impact on their families and loved ones. I am still in awe of how ill-prepared families, society, and the medical system are to confront these serious conditions that rob us of our independence and identities.

*

Now, from my window at home, I watch the Intracoastal Waterway — the waves that the wind and boats make. Boats drift past in slow procession, their wakes bending the light, breaking it into trembling shards. Some afternoons, the sun strikes the water with such brilliance that it feels less like reflection than revelation, a sudden glimpse of something beyond matter. It blinds and then it softens, reminding me that everything luminous also fades.

I know this is not the final harbor, only a resting place along the way. My journey, like every tide, will return to its origin. In the end, all roads bend toward the first compass in the soil, the sky, and the voices of Spain. For now, I wait here — between sea and sky, between departure and return. With a pilgrim's acceptance: that every life is a circle, and every circle finds its way home.

288

Part IV.
WITNESS TO HISTORY

"Never be afraid to make some noise and get into good, necessary trouble."

—John Lewis

Chapter 9: This Strange Country called America

Anti-Vietnam War Marches

New York City, 1970

I was back in New York City. The details blur now, but some visual memories and feelings remain sharp.

On May 4, 1970, thirteen students were shot (four of them fatally) at Kent State University in Ohio by National Guardsmen during a protest of U.S. involvement in the Vietnam War and the recent U.S. incursions into neutral Cambodia. In the days leading up to the violence, tensions were already escalating. There had been more minor clashes between construction workers and anti-war demonstrators.

As a show of sympathy for the slain students, New York City's Republican mayor at the time, John Lindsay, ordered all flags at City Hall to be flown at half-staff on May 8.

I joined a massive demonstration in the middle of Manhattan, swept up in a river of humanity. Thousands of us marched: young and old, students and professionals. We moved quickly and purposefully, our footsteps against the steel and concrete of the city. It wasn't anger that filled the air; it was urgency. A collective desperation to be heard. To stop the madness.

Somewhere in Midtown, the current of the march slowed. A ripple of tension passed through the crowd. Up ahead, a group of construction workers had descended from a scaffolding. Their hard hats gleamed under the spring sun. A few of them clutched baseball bats, fists tight, eyes burning with indignation. They weren't just angry; they were ready for a fight.

For a surreal moment, the protest seemed poised to erupt into violence. I thought, *this is absurd. The construction workers were only a handful, and the crowd numbered in the thousands.* They were brave, but foolish.

However, the organizers quickly stepped between the two groups, urging them to remain calm. Voices rose, but no blows were exchanged. The march continued, flowing around the workers like water around a rock.

Those men had a kind of courage that's difficult to understand. To them, we were the enemies of their country. They weren't cartoon villains or mindless thugs. They were proud, working-class Americans who fiercely believed that their nation was under threat. To them, we were traitors, naive idealists who didn't understand sacrifice or duty. They were defending what they believed was right.

And that's what broke my heart.

Because we weren't so different; we were both trying to protect something precious. But they had been fed the story that Vietnam was a noble crusade against communism and that anyone who opposed it was un-American. They hadn't seen what I had seen. They hadn't sat in that lecture hall in Boston, watching humanity torn apart on a projector screen.

What I saw that day turned out to be only the prelude to a larger confrontation. The Hard Hat Riot erupted on May 8, 1970. On that Friday in history, about 400 construction workers and roughly 800 office workers attacked nearly 1,000 anti-war demonstrators affiliated with the student strike of 1970. The demonstrators were protesting the Kent State shootings and the Vietnam War following President Nixon's April 30 announcement of the invasion of Cambodia.

Some construction workers carried American flags and chanted, "U.S.A., all the way!" and "America, love it or leave it!"

Anti-war protesters responded with chants of "Peace now!"

The riot first broke out near Wall Street in Lower Manhattan, quickly escalating into a mob scene involving more than 20,000 people. It led to a siege of New York City Hall, an attack on the conservative Pace University, and lasted more than three hours. Around a hundred people, including seven police officers, were injured. No one was killed, but many students were seriously hurt. Six people were arrested, but only one was a construction worker associated with the violence.

In the days that followed, President Nixon invited the hard hat leaders to the White House and accepted a hard hat as a gift. I remember thinking: *What a tragedy. Not just the war itself but the way it divides people who should be allies.*

The incident partly explains the political divide between conservative-leaning working-class Americans who support the Republican Party even when it conflicts with their interests. On the other hand, working-class Europeans tend to favor socialism and its policies. We were all victims of the same system, manipulated, polarized, and used. And in the middle of it all was Vietnam, a beautiful country burned to ash, with many thousands killed or maimed for life.

That march didn't stop the war. But it helped shape me. It taught me that bearing witness isn't enough. You have to speak. You have to stand up even when others don't understand, even when they hate you for it.

Many years later, while working for the U.S. government and treating hundreds of veterans with invisible wounds

(PTSD, depression, and other mental health injuries) one thing struck me. How many people had been morally destroyed. They carried an overwhelming guilt for what they had done on the battlefield and beyond. It was difficult for them to even speak of it.

I remember one deeply distressed young man, just returned from Iraq, who said to me, "I know for sure that God will never forgive me."

That, too, is the legacy of war. Decisions made in the chaos of conflict etched a moral injury into the soul.

The kind of injury no medal, parade, or apology can heal.

Washington, D.C.

Some time later, I found myself in Washington, D.C. The heart of the machine. Nixon was president and the Vietnam War raged like a fever that wouldn't break. I wasn't there for a protest that day. I was just walking. It was a quiet afternoon; my steps were aimless, but my thoughts were heavy.

The city felt like a strange blend of majesty and menace. White marble buildings gleamed beneath a pale sky, symbols of power and purpose. But beneath the surface, something darker pulsed — a tension that I could feel in my bones. Guards stood on every corner. Helicopters hovered in the distance. The weight of surveillance was everywhere. I wasn't paranoid. This was real. It was the D.C. of wiretaps, blocklists, and sealed rooms.

Walking past the White House gates, I stopped and stared for a long while. There it was. The place where decisions were made that sent young men to die, that tore apart families in both America and Vietnam. Behind those walls, a president sat in comfort and power while the world outside trembled with protest, grief, and rage.

As I stood there, I didn't feel rage. I felt profound sorrow. For the soldiers who believed. For the Vietnamese who suffered. For the working men in hard hats who couldn't see through the propaganda. For all of us caught in the tide of history, trying to make sense of a world that no longer made sense.

I thought: *This is not leadership. This is groupthink. Delusion.*

I realized something then: true patriotism is not unquestioning loyalty. It's asking hard questions. It's standing in the streets when your heart breaks over what your country is doing. It's daring to hope that compassion can still win out over violence.

I walked on. And with every step, I felt more certain about the kind of doctor I wanted to be, the kind of man, and the kind of citizen. Not one ruled by fear. Not silenced by cynicism. Someone who could hold space for pain, for contradiction, and for healing.

Not long after, I saw a small group of students on a corner, handing out anti-war pamphlets to passing cars. They were young, barely more than teenagers. They seemed earnest, hopeful, and maybe a little nervous. You could see in their eyes that they were doing something they believed in, something that mattered. There were no chants, no signs, just leaflets, and the hope that a single piece of paper might change a mind.

Then a car slowed.

A man leaned out the window with red-faced fury. He screamed something I couldn't make out, but the anger was unmistakable. Then, in one quick, awful motion, he threw the contents of his coffee cup in the students' faces and sped off. It wasn't just coffee. It was contempt.

One of the students staggered back, shocked and soaked, but didn't retaliate. Another wiped his face, calmly picked up the wet pamphlets from the sidewalk, and started again. As if to say, "We keep going."

I stood there, frozen and feeling shame, not for them, but for us. For a society that had allowed this kind of violence to grow. For the blind cruelty masquerading as patriotism. For the fear that had twisted neighbor against neighbor.

I had seen images of limbs blown off in war. I had seen fury in the eyes of construction workers. But that cup of coffee somehow hit just as hard. It laid bare how fragile our democracy was, how easily hatred could be stirred, and how much courage it took to stand still and offer truth without raising a fist.

That afternoon, I saw those same students being chased by goons, colossal muscle men, plainclothes police officers or FBI agents, who leapt from unmarked cars to beat and arrest them. But the students were younger, leaner, and outran the goons. I felt relieved.

A few days later, I saw something that shook me differently. It was near a park just off campus. The war protests were everywhere by then, like brushfires flaring up across the country. That day, a handful of students were handing out leaflets again — their movements quick, their eyes alert. They knew the risks. We all did.

It happened fast. An unmarked car screeched to a halt at the curb. The doors flew open, and two massive men jumped out. They weren't in uniform, but they were clearly law enforcement or working for someone who was. They moved with purpose. With violence.

The students scattered and ran like startled deer. The goons gave chase, snarling with fists clenched. For a moment, I couldn't breathe. It was like watching a nightmare in broad daylight.

The kids were quicker. Smarter. They darted between parked cars, jumped fences, and slipped into alleys. One of them, barely older than twenty, turned his head as he ran and for a split second, we locked eyes. He wasn't afraid. He was alive. On fire with purpose. Heavy and angry, the goons eventually gave up, panting and frustrated. They hurled curses into the wind and stomped to their car.

I stood there, heart racing, watching the students vanish into the city and felt relief. A deep, unexpected wave of it. Not because the danger had passed but because the spirit wasn't broken. These young people were the conscience of the country. They weren't fighting with fists or bullets but with ideas, with persistence, with their bodies.

It was terrifying to see how easily power could be abused, how quickly the machinery of the state turned against its people. But it was also clarifying. This wasn't just about Vietnam anymore. It was about truth, dissent, and the right to speak without being beaten for it.

I knew I was on the right side.

Bomb Threats at the VA

During the initial months of 1995, I became entangled in a rapidly intensifying crisis that I barely comprehended at the time. Hired by the Department of Veterans Affairs to oversee an outpatient psychiatric clinic, I worked in a plain, boxy building without windows in Riviera Beach, Florida. It was a rented space, temporary, and deeply uninspiring. The top brass VA leaders were at the new West Palm Beach VA hospital, preparing for its opening later that June. We were left behind in the shadows.

From my first weeks there, I observed unsettling undercurrents. Many of our patients were veterans of different wars and openly voiced racism, sometimes without even a hint of shame. One Black cardiologist was bad-mouthed so relentlessly by patients that he was eventually pushed out. There was tension everywhere between patients and staff, between the Clinic doctors and the VA leadership, between what was said publicly and what simmered in private conversations.

It was around March 1995 that the bomb threats started.

At first, it seemed like an anomaly, a sick joke. But then the calls became routine, once, sometimes twice a week. Each time, the protocol was the same: evacuate the building, wait outside under the punishing Florida sun while bomb-sniffing German Shepherds swept through the empty rooms, when the police declared it safe, trudge back in (uneasy and exhausted), wonder if next time the dogs might miss something.

The threats raised an unsettling question: was someone trying to scare us or save us?

One encounter stays with me more than any other. A veteran from Port St. Lucie, a small town just north of West Palm Beach, came to see me, visibly anxious and desperate. He poured out a terrifying narrative. He and his friends believed federal authorities were preparing to confiscate their weapons. In response, they had laid out their guns across kitchen tables, ready to defend their homes against a phantom government assault. He warned that thousands of Chinese policemen would soon occupy American cities in a full-blown foreign invasion. He insisted this was just around the corner.

I tried to reason with him, grounding our conversation in facts, but it was like trying to hold back a flood with bare hands. His fear wasn't logical. It was visceral, immediate, and contagious among the network of veterans he knew.

Conspiracy theories had found fertile soil here, nourished by the early growth of internet forums and AM radio. Rumors even floated through the grapevine that Timothy McVeigh himself had passed through Florida, connecting with veteran groups north of West Palm Beach. Whether that was true or not, I'll never know.

But the proximity of it all still troubles me: the bomb threats, the fear in that veteran's eyes, the fraying edge between reality and delusion. Only weeks later, on April 19, 1995, McVeigh would detonate a truck bomb outside the Alfred P. Murrah Federal Building in Oklahoma City, killing 168 people, including 19 children.

I sometimes wonder if our clinic was a possible target. Did McVeigh initially consider attacking the VA in Florida before setting his plans to focus on a larger, more symbolic structure? Maybe the idea of attacking a facility providing care for veterans was too much, even for him. Or perhaps his ambition grew and he sought a target that would make headlines around the world.

The truth is lost to history. But the mood of the time with the paranoia, the rage, the sense that America was turning against itself was unmistakable. I lived inside it, if only for a short while, watching from the front row as fear hardened into hatred, and words turned, eventually, into violence.

9/11

People often say that what matters most is not what happens to you, but how you respond to it. That idea applies painfully well to America's response to the terrorist attacks of September 11, 2001.

That morning, I was working in Miami at a VA out-patient rehabilitation program for veterans with substance-use disorders. Shortly before nine o'clock, I heard shouting from the day room. A few patients had been watching television. Their voices carried urgency and fear.

When I walked in, I saw a plane crashing into one of the Twin Towers of the World Trade Center. My first instinct was to search for a rational explanation. Years earlier, a plane had struck the Empire State Building by accident. I assumed pilot error. A tragic mistake.

Seventeen minutes later, a second plane hit the other tower. At that moment, there was no doubt. This was deliberate.

We later learned that nineteen terrorists had hijacked four commercial airplanes. Two were flown into the Twin Towers. One struck the Pentagon. The fourth crashed in rural Pennsylvania after passengers fought back. Nearly three thousand people were killed. Thousands more were injured. Firefighters and police officers died in numbers never seen before in American history. Estimated economic damage ran into the hundreds of billions. Long-term health consequences continue to this day.

The shock was universal and the world was sympathetic to America. That was inevitable but what followed was not.

Instead of pausing, the country rushed forward. Grief turned quickly into anger, which demanded action. Reflection gave way to urgency and fear replaced judgment. The nation wanted justice; no, it wanted revenge. But vengeance is a dangerous compass. It points not to wisdom, not to truth, but to the easiest target.

The United States declared a "global war on terror." Over the next two decades, wars and conflicts directly linked to that decision resulted in an estimated four and a half million deaths worldwide. Four and a half million lives — and probably more — were lost as a consequence of the choices that followed 9/11.

I believed then, and still think now, that the response choices and the consequences were worse than the attack itself.

Terrorism should have been treated as an international criminal enterprise, which would have required international cooperation, intelligence sharing, police investigations, and a careful study of root causes. It would have required patience, listening, and learning new things about the world. It would not have satisfied public rage or the political ambition keen to exploit this tragedy. It would not have made leaders look more manly or decisive on television.

The government chose war.

The first target was Afghanistan, where Osama bin Laden was believed to be under Taliban protection. I opposed the invasion but accepted it as inevitable. I assumed it would be brief but it was not.

Afghanistan is one of the poorest countries in the world and has a long history of defeating foreign powers. It is often called the "graveyard of empires." The British failed there. The Soviets failed there. The United States would fail there, too.

The invasion began in 2001 to dismantle al-Qaeda and remove the Taliban. A new government was installed. Nation-building followed but there was no coherent long-term strategy and no realistic plan for withdrawal. The war dragged on for nearly twenty years.

In 2021, after enormous human and financial costs, the United States withdrew. The Afghan government collapsed almost immediately. The Taliban returned to power. The exit was chaotic and humiliating. The outcome echoed Vietnam: a guerrilla war cannot be won against an enemy rooted in its own land, supported — willingly or not — by its own population.

Millions of Afghans were left behind in despair. Countless civilians were killed or displaced. An entire generation grew up knowing nothing but war.

The United States then turned to Iraq, claiming it possessed weapons of mass destruction. UN inspectors searched the country and came back empty-handed. But absence is hard to prove, and fear is easy to sell. "What if?" became enough. What if they had them? What if a mushroom cloud appeared over New York or Washington? The administration blurred the line between fact and speculation until fear itself became the evidence.

And so, the drums of war began to thunder.

I remember the flags. They were everywhere. They flew from car windows, hung off porches, and were stitched onto backpacks. Patriotism had become a fever, and questioning the war was to brand yourself un-American.

The decision to invade was reckless. I remember agreeing with a young senator from Illinois, Barack Obama, when he warned against "dumb wars." This was one of them. If Iraq did not have weapons of mass destruction, there was no justification for invasion. If it did, sending young Americans into that danger would have been even more irresponsible.

I was the only one in my neighborhood who didn't fly a flag. Instead, I put a sign in my car window that read:

WAR IS NOT THE ANSWER

This is a slogan in the form of a window sticker I received from the American Friends Service Committee (AFSC), an organization founded in 1917 by American Quakers. The organization is committed to promoting peace, providing humanitarian aid, and advocating for social justice. And they are right. The cost of the war? Incalculable.

War Is Not the Answer. I believed it then. I believe it now. War was not the answer to the 9/11 terrorist attack.

The war that followed was not just; it was a catastrophe in every way and a moral failure. The Iraq War resulted in far more deaths than the attacks it aimed to avenge. The terrorist attacks on 9/11 killed 2,996 people. In response, the Iraq War caused even more loss of life. Over 27,000 U.S. and Coalition soldiers were killed or wounded.

More than 100,000 Iraqi innocent civilians, including mothers, children, and elders died, caught in the crossfire. Estimates such as the Lancet survey and Opinion Research Business placed the total Iraqi death toll between 392,000 and 1.1 million.

The war also led to a humanitarian crisis, displacing millions and destabilizing the entire region. And the damage didn't stop there.

Amid Iraq's chaos, ISIS emerged, a group so brutal and fanatical it made Al-Qaeda seem restrained by comparison. Their rise triggered another war in Iraq (2013–2017), resulting in over 155,000 additional deaths and pushing the Middle East further into despair. Iran also gained substantial influence, boosted by the power vacuum left by America.

At home, trust in the government collapsed. President Bush's popularity plummeted. Yet, no American administration has ever fully acknowledged the scale of the disaster or taken responsibility for it.

Civil liberties eroded quickly. Congress passed the USA Patriot Act. Surveillance expanded. Judicial oversight weakened. The NSA was granted sweeping powers to monitor communications without warrants. Privacy became condition-al. Fear and patriotism justified everything.

America after 9/11 lives with a permanent sense of doom and anxiety. Suspicion toward immigrants grew, especially toward people from Muslim and Arab countries. Hate crimes increased. Mosques and temples were attacked. Sikhs were assaulted for wearing turbans. At airports, everyone became a suspect. Shoes came off. Luggage was searched. Bodies were scanned. Fear became routine.

America before 9/11 felt freer.

It could have been different.

Cicero once said that the true work of age is judgment, reflection, and wisdom. Leaders, too, are called to this higher ground. A government should elevate and guide its people rather than pander to their rawest emotions. It should stabilize the nation when grief and rage threaten to blind it. Instead, our leaders matched fury with fury, fear with fear, until reason was drowned out in the noise. That is why war is not the answer. War arises from reaction rather than reflection. War may seem like clarity, but it only causes chaos. When leaders follow the passions of the crowd instead of guiding them, they lead us all into disaster.

The lesson is as urgent today as it was back then: when anger demands action, wisdom must whisper for restraint. When the drums of war sound, we should ask not "What can we destroy?" but "What must we protect?"

Above all, we must remember that a nation's worth is not in how quickly it retaliates, but in how deeply it thinks before acting. It should consider both the moral and political dimensions, as well as the short-term and long-term consequences.

A nation lost its moral compass. Deception replaced truth. Force replaced restraint and the consequences are still unfolding.

Abad

My last name, ABAD, has always preceded me.

It arrives before I do — on forms, on screens, on security lists, on the brief pause that follows when someone reads it silently and recalibrates. Abad. Four letters. Clean. Ancient. And, in the United States, it is endlessly misunderstood.

For most of my life here, many have assumed it is Arabic. After 9/11, that assumption became anything but innocent. A name, I learned, can become a question mark. Or worse, a suspicion. Veterans came to my office to question me, to make sure I was not Muslim. My last name sounded suspicious to them. I considered changing it. I did not. But the thought crossed my mind more than once.

After 9/11, the world did not simply change in public ways. It changed privately. Fear seeped into ordinary encounters, into glances and pauses, into how people were read before they were known. I did not feel this shift all at once. It revealed itself slowly, through something as simple and enduring as my last name.

The 9/11 attacks altered borders, policies, and wars. They also changed perception.

From that moment on, identity itself became suspect and some of us learned that history could follow us quietly, written not on our actions, but on our names.

I have often wondered — quietly, without drama — how many databases I have passed through, how many screens have lingered a second longer because of those four letters. I have never been accused of anything. But I have felt the temperature change. The pause. The extra glance. The bureaucratic hesitation that has nothing to do with me as a person and everything to do with a sound that triggers an association.

It is a strange thing to be misread by your own name.

What makes the irony almost poetic is that Abad is not a name of threat, but of care. It does not mean warrior, conqueror, or zealot. It means abbot. Father. Guardian. A man entrusted with the care of others.

The word comes from abbas, in late Latin, itself drawn from the Aramaic abba — father. It was a title before it became a surname. A designation for those who presided over monasteries, who kept order, offered refuge, listened to confession, mediated conflict, and held communities together in times when life was precarious and the world unforgiving.

In medieval Spain, where my name took root, an Abad was not a man of spectacle. He was a man of structure. Someone associated with an abbey, under its protection, or in its service. Over time, the title hardened into inheritance. The role dissolved, but the name remained.

Spain, of course, was never simple. Latin, Arabic, Hebrew, Christian, Muslim, Jewish — all braided together for centuries. Words crossed borders the way people did. It is true that in Arabic, similar sounds, ʻAbd, ʻAbbād, mean devotion or service to God. Different roots, different grammars but a shared gravity: humility, obligation, surrender to something larger than the self.

That shared meaning should have united, not divided. But history rarely respects etymology.

In America, nuance does not travel well. After 9/11, names were flattened. Accents sharpened into liabilities. Complexity collapsed into fear. Islamophobia did not require accuracy; it required only resemblance. To sound "foreign" was enough. To sound Arab was already too much.

For decades, I suspect my name has lived a parallel life apart from me — circulating quietly through systems, tagged not by who I am, but by what it resembles. I have no proof of this. But one develops a certain intuition when one has lived long enough at the margins of belonging.

What saddens me is not the inconvenience. It is the betrayal of meaning.

Abad does not belong to violence. It belongs to care. It does not signify extremism. It signifies stewardship. It does not speak of domination but of responsibility.

If anything, the name has always suited my life more than I realized. I became a physician. A psychiatrist. A listener. I served as a caregiver for individuals whose minds had wandered and fractured due to immense suffering. I worked with veterans, the uninsured, immigrants, and the forgotten. I stood not at altars, but in clinics. I was not in monasteries but rather in waiting rooms. Yet the posture was similar: attend, contain, protect.

Perhaps that is the final irony. A name misread as dangerous belonged, all along, to a man devoted to healing.

I no longer feel the need to defend it. Names, like people, survive misunderstanding. They outlast fear.

COVID-19 and BLM, 2020

I lived in Boca Raton, in a gated community, then. In early 2020, when the virus began its silent spread, I remember looking out at the wide lawns, the sun-blanched sidewalks, and the empty clubhouse where neighbors once greeted each other with coffee and small talk. Overnight, it felt as if someone had frozen time.

Everyone wore masks. When we walked outside, people invariably moved in one direction, away from another, as if fearing the wind might carry more than air. Grocery delivery trucks became a lifeline. Telehealth became the only door through which I saw many of my patients. As a psychiatrist, I took their histories in pixelated frames, comforting them behind the computer screen, while the real world outside seemed to crumble.

Death was no longer an abstract possibility. It became ordinary. The U.S. recorded roughly 3.38 million deaths, about

529,000 more than in 2019. Among them, at least 350,831 died with COVID-19 listed as the underlying cause. The pandemic turned the familiar streets into silent graveyards. Nursing-home residents vanished behind locked doors, sometimes dying alone. My patients lost their parents. Children lost grandparents. Entire lifetimes ended in isolation.

We clung to fear and what precautions we could manage: masks, distance, curfews, and closed businesses. The only shield we had before vaccines arrived was isolation. And yet, isolation itself became a weight; grief was compressed in small rooms, in endless nights, and in phone calls that replaced visits. I saw quiet sorrow deepen like shadows beneath eyes. I heard the unbearable hush of homes made empty.

But then summer came, and with it a different kind of tremor.

On May 25, a cell phone video captured a murder: a white police officer pressing his knee on the neck of a Black man, George Floyd, who pleaded, "I can't breathe." The video stirred something ancient: a grief buried for generations, a rage long held captive in silence, and a collective ache for justice.

In days, cities filled with people, rivers of faces and voices joining in sorrow and hope. Within months, the most significant protest movement in modern American history was underway. Some estimates suggest between 15 and 26 million individuals in the U.S. alone joined a protest at some point that summer.

Signs reading "Black Lives Matter", "No justice, no peace", "Defund the police" multiplied. The streets echoed with chants, grief, memory, and determination.

I watched on television, but also heard it in prayer calls, in neighborhood longings, in the hushed hopes of immigrant patients who had never felt safe in their own skin. COVID-19 had exposed who had shelter and who didn't; who could lock their doors and wait, and who had to show up to work to survive. The virus and injustice converged into a single test.

At times, it felt like the country was collapsing on its lungs, on its conscience, on its memory. I asked myself, *is this the end of the promise?*

And yet, even then, I saw acts of grace: neighbors bringing groceries to elders, volunteers sewing masks, people checking on each other — on the phone, from a safe distance, with a soft "I'm here." Courts kept working. Journalists kept asking questions. Clinics kept offering help. The rule of law, though stretched, did not disappear.

In the loneliness of tele-appointments, I heard despair. In the protests, I saw hope. In the grief of loss, I sensed a longing for rebirth.

I came to America expecting freedom. Instead, I discovered what freedom truly is: the burden of choice and the weight of what follows. Free not to live as you were born but free to choose who you become. And with that freedom, you inherit responsibility: to think, to care, to speak, and to act.

In 2020, I witnessed death. I witnessed pain. I witnessed fear. And I witnessed awakening.

That year bent the compass of the world. And quietly, painfully, it demanded that we rebuild. We had to rebuild, brick by brick and act by act, starting anew.

America in 2025-2026

I write these lines with a heavy heart and a clear mind. I have lived long enough to recognize a pattern when it returns. Fear always comes back wearing new clothes. I have seen how fear breeds tyranny, how confusion invites manipulation, and how democracies often crumble not by invasion from abroad but by erosion from within. They weaken from within, slowly, while people reassure themselves that this moment is temporary.

When Donald Trump returned to Washington for a second term, it did not feel like a lawful transition. It felt like a seizure. Executive orders arrived in waves, faster than the public could absorb them. Agencies bent or broke. Congress stayed quiet. Courts objected at times, but rulings were ignored.

"What does he want?" a friend asked me one night.

"Power," I said. "Unchecked power." I struggled to understand the speed of it all with baffling announcements, shocking executive orders, and a hostility toward institutions at the core of our democracy.

I had seen this rhythm before. In Franco's Spain, where laws were decorations and fear did the real governing. And again after 9/11, when shock turned into urgency, and urgency turned into permission. Once a nation accepts that emergency overrides restraint, the emergency never ends. It only finds new targets.

At first, the obsession was immigration. ICE agents appeared everywhere. Not just at borders. Outside courthouses. Clinics. Schools. Workplaces. People with permits. People with pending cases. People who had done what the law required. They were taken anyway.

"They grabbed him when he went to court," a patient told me.

"She was arrested at work," another said.

"He didn't even get to call his lawyer."

In Minneapolis, an American woman, Renee Good, tried to drive away from ICE agents. She was shot three times through her car window and killed. The video spread within hours. The administration called her a domestic terrorist. No proof. The facts on video said otherwise.

"They're blaming the dead," a colleague said to me.

"That's how you know the truth no longer matters," I replied.

The policy was sold as law and order. What I saw was intimidation dressed as governance. A message delivered with force: I can reach into your life. I can erase you. I can do it again.

Then came the bending of the justice system.

When James Comey was indicted, it was not handled with restraint. The president celebrated publicly and hinted at more targets. Other names followed — political opponents, critics, regulators. Inside the Department of Justice, career prosecutors raised concerns. Outside, crowds cheered.

That moment told me more than any speech. When prosecution becomes performance, loyalty becomes safer than truth.

I know that atmosphere well. I have lived under systems where suspicion is praised and innocence must be proven. Surveillance lists grow quickly. Innocent people get caught. Once the machinery exists, it does not limit itself to the guilty.

The pattern spread. Education was attacked. Universities were pressured. Science was politicized. Research became suspect if it did not fit the leader's story. Public health agencies were undermined. Expertise was treated as betrayal. Foreign aid became transactional. Compassion became conditional. Even the Federal Reserve felt public intimidation. Independence became inconvenient. Veterans' services and civil agencies were shaken by cuts and purges, often faster than anyone could assess the damage.

In every drift toward authoritarian rule, the first enemies are the referees: judges, teachers, scientists, journalists, civil servants. Anyone who says, Slow down. Prove it.

This is how democracies change shape. People lower their voices. They keep their heads down. They learn that the law is no longer a shield. It is a weapon held by someone else.

Even as I recognize these parallels, I remain anchored in my own moral perspective — a liberal democratic commitment shaped by exile, psychiatry, and a lifetime spent studying the delicate machinery of human dignity.

Reading Katherine Stewart's Money, Lies, and God helped me connect the dots. This was not one man acting alone. It was an ecosystem — wealth, media, ideology, and power — working to hollow out democracy. The strategy was old and brutal: Discredit truth, break institutions, control education, turn citizens against one another, rule through fear and demand loyalty.

Chaos makes people cling to anyone who promises order — even when he is the one creating the chaos. Some religious groups joined in. They traded compassion for power. That may be the deepest loss of all. When faith becomes a weapon, it ceases to be sacred.

Understanding these roots brings a measure of relief. It helps explain the fracture without dehumanizing those caught in it. It reminds us that fear and confusion can make even good people vulnerable to the allure of strongmen — a truth as old as history, from Spain in 1936 to America in 2025.

I have lived too many years in exile to believe that darkness always wins. I have seen democracies fracture and heal. I have heard cruelty shout and seen conscience whisper through the cracks.

America is wounded but not defeated.

The rule of law still lives in courtrooms. Scientific truth still burns in laboratories and classrooms. Ordinary citizens still carry quiet courage. The Constitution, though battered, still stands. And history has a way of testing a nation only to reveal the strength of its foundation.

I do not believe this administration will dismantle America as easily as it imagines. The habit of liberty runs too deep. The muscle memory of justice is still alive. And when democracy is threatened, defenders often rise from unexpected places.

I still bet on America — not out of innocence but out of long memory.

Because in the end, my faith is not in leaders but in the moral courage of Americans who refuse to surrender their conscience.

When that moral compass wakes up, it does not shout or chant. It moves steadily. And that is how nations find their way back from the edge.

The Two Americas

I did not fall in love with the America of wealth or power. My devotion was to the America of light — the America of the spirit. It was an America that believed in human dignity, second chances, equal justice under the law. A country founded not on blood or ancestry but on a daring idea: that a human being could be the author of their own life, that no king, church, or general could claim ownership over another soul.

That was the America I sought when I first arrived.

I admired the country that passed courageous laws not because they were easy but because they were right. I admired the America that expanded rights for women, opened doors to people of color, and began — slowly, imperfectly — listening to the voices of gay and trans people who had been pushed to the margins for generations. I admired a country capable of political evolution. A society willing to revise itself.

I saw universities where thought could breathe freely, where physics could flirt with infinity and philosophy could question everything without fear. Questions were not seen as threats but as invitations. I admired the quiet courage of its scientists, working late into the night, searching for knowledge that might heal or illuminate. I admired the audacity of its astronauts, who looked at the stars and saw not distance but destiny.

And I admired something even rarer: grace in victory. After wars were fought and enemies defeated, America extended a hand to rebuild what had been destroyed. It helped Europe and Japan rise from ruins. That willingness to rebuild former enemies seemed to me a moral triumph greater than any military one. The world followed America not only because of its might but because of its vision.

This was how the Cold War was won: not just with weapons but with belief. The belief that freedom would draw people across borders. That democracy could offer something communism could not: the dignity of choice. The Eastern Bloc cracked not from invasion but from interior longing. A system that forbids dreams cannot endure forever.

But there is another America, its darker twin. I have seen it too.

It is the America filled with resentment and fear of the foreign-born. The America that wraps itself in flags while confusing cruelty with strength and nostalgia with truth. It mocks the accented voice, blames the poor for their poverty, and prefers regression to progress. It chooses indoctrination over education, vengeance over justice. It dreams of walls at borders, between races, and between truths. "Us" against "them," even when the border runs straight through our own families.

These two Americas coexist. They do not cancel each other out; they collide, like tectonic plates, creating fractures and political earthquakes.

For a long time, I saw this clash primarily as a battle between good and evil: those who defended human dignity versus those who trampled it. Then I grew older, and the political darkness of recent years deepened. I watched America tilt toward a new form of authoritarian temptation wearing the language of patriotism.

I began to feel the same unease I had once felt in Spain.

I needed a way to understand people who held political ideologies contrary to mine without hating them, and to resist political misinformation and lies without losing compassion.

Jonathan Haidt's work gave me a language. He argues that human beings do not start with reason; we start with intuition. We feel first, and explain later. We are divided not because one side is moral and the other immoral but because we draw from different moral foundations — different "moral taste buds" shaped by our histories, our fears, and our tribes.

Suddenly, the rift between conservatives and liberals looked painfully familiar. It resembled the divide that tore Spain apart in the 1930s. Republicans and Francoists lived in the same land, spoke the same language, yet inhabited different moral worlds. Each side judged the other not only as wrong but as dangerous and illegitimate.

In today's United States, I see the same pattern.

The liberal left draws most strongly on compassion, fairness, and liberty. The conservative right emphasizes loyalty, order, and the sacred.

Each side believes it is defending what is most precious; each suspects the other of madness or malice.

Haidt helped me recognize what age had already begun to teach me: good people can be divided by politics and religion not because they lack morality but because they draw from different moral wells.

Understanding this does not remove the danger of extremism but it does make dialogue possible and even allows for some measure of peace. It allows us to say: I think you are wrong, perhaps dangerously wrong, but I will not erase your humanity.

Yet understanding the psychological roots of division does not mean all positions are equal. Some moral visions lead toward justice and human flourishing; others toward cruelty and degradation.

My own moral home lies firmly within the liberal democratic tradition —a worldview shaped by freedom, truth, and the intrinsic dignity of each person. From that vantage point, I cannot stay silent about what I have seen in recent years. Because the danger we face today is not simply "one more moral tribe among many."

The movement embodied by Trump is not rooted in a different moral foundation; it is rooted in something thinner: resentment, vengeance, spectacle, and power for its own sake. His willingness to endorse extrajudicial killings of suspected traffickers, or to consider pardoning a former president of Honduras convicted of drug trafficking simply because he offered praise, reveals a worldview stripped of moral restraint. These are not conservative values. They are the politics of appetite and domination unburdened by ethics.

This is why I see the current moment as morally urgent.

Not because one party is always right and the other always wrong but because one side has begun to abandon the moral foundations that make democracy possible.

Even so, I take comfort in what this new understanding offers.

Seeing our conflict as a clash of moral foundations does not weaken our resolve; it strengthens it. It reminds us that persuasion requires humility, empathy, and a willingness to speak in the moral language of the other side. It reassures us that a moral vision grounded in truth and compassion can still cut through the fog of fear and propaganda.

This insight calms me. It tells me that America is not simply divided into the righteous and the damned. It is filled with frightened, confused, and morally bewildered human beings — just as Spain once was and just as all nations are when their foundations shake.

Recognizing this helps me resist the temptation to dehumanize those whose politics I find repellent. It allows me to condemn policies without despising people. It keeps my heart from hardening even as my judgment grows sharper.

And so, in this season of turmoil, I hold to a quiet conviction: If we can understand the moral foundations of those we oppose, we can begin to heal the fractures that politics alone cannot mend.

We can speak across the canyon rather than shout into it. We can defend democracy without surrendering to hatred. We can stand against authoritarianism without becoming fanatics ourselves.

Perhaps we can help America find its way back to its better self: the America of light that first drew me here, the America that rebuilds, revises, and grows, even after wandering in darkness.

Because in the end, democracy is not built on perfect agreement. It is built on the willingness to understand, to restrain power, and to honor the dignity that lies buried inside every moral worldview, even the ones we reject.

That dignity still lives in America. And it is worth fighting for.

Part V:
FACING MORTALITY

"The thought of death is the key to life."

—Søren Kierkegaard

Chapter 10:
Before It's Too Late

"It is not death that a man should fear, but he should fear never beginning to live."

—Marcus Aurelius

Everybody Has to Die

Out of the many notable men and women who died in 2025, several have placed an imprint on my life.

They came from different worlds — science, politics, faith, and the arts — but together they marked an era. I have lived my entire life hearing about them, watching them work, admiring their achievements, their persistence, and sometimes their contradictions. Their deaths feel less like a series of isolated losses and more like a slow curtain lowering on a generation.

Jane Goodall devoted her life to studying chimpanzees. Through years of patient observation, she changed how we understand animals and ourselves. I watched her work countless times in documentaries, interviews, and lectures. What impressed me most was not only her science but her way of being. She listened carefully. She watched without haste. She spoke with humility. She taught us that attention itself can be a moral act. Even late in life, when travel became difficult, she kept teaching responsibility toward the living world.

James D. Watson, co-discoverer of the structure of DNA, helped unlock the biological code that shapes every human life. His legacy, like most human legacies, was imperfect and complex. Yet his scientific contribution transformed medicine, genetics, and modern biology. Entire fields grew from that discovery.

Nuno Loureiro worked far from the spotlight in the demanding world of plasma physics and fusion research. His work belonged to that quiet frontier where science looks toward long-term solutions (new sources of energy and a more profound understanding of the universe) often without recognition or applause. A former classmate recently murdered him at home after a bizarre and senseless mass shooting at Brown University.

Jim Lovell represented another kind of greatness. As commander of Apollo 13 he helped turn a mission that should have ended in disaster into one of survival. His legacy was not one of bravado but one full of discipline, teamwork, and clear thinking under pressure.

Pope Francis led the Catholic Church with an insistence on humility, mercy, and concern for the poor. He spoke often of conscience and moral responsibility in a fractured world. Whether one agreed with him or not, he reminded us that authority can speak softly and that leadership does not require cruelty.

Politics left a heavy imprint.

Dick Cheney shaped American foreign policy during the years after 9/11, marked by fear and conflict, including the wars in Afghanistan and Iraq. His influence was decisive and controversial. Jean-Marie Le Pen represented another face of political life — nationalism fueled by anger and exclusion. Their careers remind us that history is not guided only by wisdom but often by fear, ambition, and ideology.

In the arts, the losses felt personal.

Robert Redford had been part of my inner landscape for decades. I watched him in *The Way We Were, Butch Cassidy and the Sundance Kid, All the President's Men*, and many other films. He carried an air of quiet resistance and moral gravity. Beyond acting, he nurtured independent cinema making space for stories that might have otherwise never been told. Gene Hackman portrayed men who were flawed, forceful, and unsettling. In *The French Connection* he gave us a character stripped of heroism and illusion. He trusted the truth of the character even when it was uncomfortable. Diane Keaton brought intelligence and vulnerability to the screen. She aged in public without apology, redefining what it meant to remain creative and relevant.

Ozzy Osbourne turned excess and inner chaos into sound. His music gave voice to generations who felt restless or unseen. He lived long enough to look back and reflect. Roberta Flack sang with restraint and emotional clarity. Her voice did not demand attention; it invited listening.

And then there was Brigitte Bardot. As a young man I was enthralled by her. Like many of my generation, I watched her films — *And God Created Woman, A Very Private Affair, Naughty Girl*, to name a few of my favorites — with fascination. She embodied beauty, rebellion, and freedom. Later, she surprised many by turning away from fame to dedicate herself fiercely to animal rights. She chose conviction over applause.

They are gone now. And many others with them.

The news has felt like a quiet farewell. Each week another name appears in the obituaries. A generation has begun to leave the stage. They are roughly my age.

Their deaths stirred something unexpected in me. Not only grief but recognition. If they have gone, then perhaps I too, am waiting in the wings — for my cue, for the final act.

What struck me most was not that they died but how long they kept working. They never truly retired from life. Goodall was still traveling and teaching gentleness when walking became difficult. Others wrote books in their eighties and launched foundations in their nineties. Anthony Hopkins, also born in 1937, is still alive and published his memoir in 2025. They stayed engaged.

If they could keep going, what excuse do I have?

For years, I wrestled with my own mind. ADHD scattered my energies — potential everywhere, roots nowhere. But mortality now stands before me not as a threat but as an honest teacher. *You may not have endless time. But you still have time*, I tell myself as I try to become more organized and productive.

The body weakens. That is unavoidable. Yet this makes health more valuable — not for appearance but for function. If I care for my body I may earn ten more years. Ten focused years. Ten years to finish the projects that have followed me like loyal shadows.

I still carry dreams. My incomplete list: to translate this book into other languages, to write other books that clarify psychiatry, medicine, and philosophy; to create films and videos that inspire, to expand mental-health care for minorities and the uninsured, to imagine a future in which technology and engineering are used more for healing and the benefit of mankind, rather than the billionaire class.

I may never see these dreams come to life. That is not the point. The point is to begin. Others will continue the work.

Some books awaken rather than instruct. *Staring at the Sun* by Irvin D. Yalom did that for me. It taught me that, when faced honestly, death can teach us how to live.

Yalom speaks of "rippling"— the way our lives extend into the lives of others. Something as simple as a word spoken, a kindness offered, a hand held in silence becomes part of someone else's story. We continue in those ripples, even when our names disappear.

Everybody has to die. No one leaves this world alive. We know this abstractly yet we rarely fully believe it because we cannot imagine our own absence or picture the world continuing without us. Perhaps the task then is not to solve death or master it but to live attentively while we are here — to notice the quiet gift of dawn and sunset, the ocean breeze on the skin, the sound of children laughing as they lose themselves in play, untouched by calculation or regret. Not everything needs to be analyzed and not every memory needs to be reopened.

What matters is whether we dare to live more honestly before that moment arrives. Whether we pause long enough to examine our lives, let go of what is not truly ours, or move closer to what gives our days meaning — for now, that choice remains.

A Farewell to the Young Wayfarer

I write to you now— the young wayfarer— who stands at the threshold of the road, uncertain before the unknown. I felt it once, too. I was that young boy in Valencia, walking sun-struck streets that smelled of tradition and possibility. But Spain felt narrow. Franco's shadow pressed down on every conversation, on every classroom, even on the dreams we did not dare to speak aloud. Patriotism felt hollow and obedience was a currency demanded in advance. There were voices trying to shape me into something safer. Each time, something within me stirred.

In the end, I chose medicine — not for prestige but for the possibility of easing human suffering. I sensed that even if I could not cure cancer or decipher schizophrenia, I could sit beside a person in pain and make them feel less alone. One human life at a time. That would be enough. And it was.

To you, young wayfarer — I offer this:

Do not grip life too tightly. What you try to control will stiffen in your hands. Be kind, but do not abandon the steering wheel of your own life. And do not wait for life to begin. It is already happening in every hesitation, in the quiet yes that rises before a decision, in the love you dare (or do not dare) to speak.

What I have learned through migrations, ambitions, failures, small miracles, and even a brush with death is simple enough to write in one breath but hard enough to live for a lifetime: you are responsible for the direction of your life. No one is coming to save you. If you walk with clarity, the universe has a way of meeting you halfway.

With time, I learned what I now pass to you, not as commandments but as a lantern to carry with you on your path:

A meaningful life does not begin with certainty. It begins with honesty. With the courage to ask: *What am I afraid of? What do I truly want? What values will I protect when no one is watching?* If you are young and unsure, listen carefully. There is no shame in not knowing. The shame is in refusing to learn. Name your hope. What remains unspoken remains unborn.

There are two choices that will shape the rest of your days: the work you give your time to and the people you share your life with. Choose a vocation that serves life, not only your résumé. Choose companions who breathe wind into your sails. Choose a partner who respects your autonomy, encourages your growth, and is not intimidated by your dreams. A relationship without freedom becomes a quiet prison. Love can both illuminate and wound. If you do not do your inner work, you will expect others to repair what you abandoned. But real love is not rescue; it is recognition. It is the meeting of two free individuals, neither of them complete. Those who love you well will never ask you to shrink so they can feel tall.

Service offers the same lesson. It is not martyrdom, and it should never be performed. It is simply the willingness to ask: *What can I offer? How can I help?*

Science changes. Religions differ. Philosophies evolve. But the essential principles endure: act with compassion. Stay curious. Cause as little harm as possible.

You will not feel complete every day. That is not failure. That is life shaping you. Some dreams will change shape. Some people you love will walk away. And you, too, will hurt others—not always by intention but sometimes by carelessness. Still, do not withdraw. Do not harden. Take responsibility and keep walking.

Stand tall when the world tries to fold you. Keep your body strong. It will carry you farther than ambition ever will.

Put small things in order: the bed, the bill, the unresolved call. Seek meaning over comfort. Comfort collapses; meaning endures. Risk the fall. Balance is learned by falling.

*

I have walked much of my life like Bosch's Wayfarer — burdened, tempted, and sometimes weary. The dog of fear nipped at my heel; the brothel of illusions beckoned from every corner. Yet still, I walked. Not perfectly. Not without regrets. But forward. And every so often, I felt the quiet presence of grace: the hand of a patient who trusted me, the voice of a friend who saw me, the unexpected kindness of a stranger. These were my lanterns.

Now it is your turn to walk. Walk steadily, young traveler. The lantern is already in your hands. It always was.

Brick by Brick

(in the spirit of Rabindranath Tagore)

We are not the dreams that visit our sleep

nor the fears that walk beside us at dawn.

We are not the distant footsteps of childhood

nor the sorrows we've learned to silence.

We are the choices we make

brick by brick, breath by breath:

rising, faltering,

beginning again.

The darkness arrives without warning.

The light must be courted with devotion.

Love is not promised;

it must be lived.

Forgiveness does not excuse;

it sets the heart free.

Joy is a dare.

And trust too.

Without them,

we wander the world

as shadows.

If we repeat what we have not healed,

let us, rewrite our story

with the ink of courage.

Too soon, we are old.

Too late, we are wise.

Still, the lamp is lit within us.

There is time

to walk toward its glow,

to step onto the sacred stage

of this unrepeatable life.

Acknowledgements

This book—like any life honestly lived—was not made alone. It rests on patience, loyalty, generosity, and love. Many people carried me, steadied me, or simply showed up when it mattered. Some did it loudly. Most did it quietly. I am grateful to all of you.

My Closest Circle

To my wife: You are my anchor and my compass—my protector, my physician, my nurse, and my mirror, day and night. No European king, president, or prime minister receives the vigilant, around-the-clock care you give me. Your strength and discipline keep our lives running. Your tenderness, often hidden beneath urgency and precision, shows me what devotion looks like in real life. You hold the details, the emergencies, the decisions, and the fatigue. You do it with courage and grit. Thank you for loving fiercely, for guarding relentlessly, and for giving your best to our family and to everyone around us.

To my son: Thank you for your loyalty, your quiet strength, and your unwavering sense of responsibility. You have supported your mother and managed her practice and properties with skill and humility. You show up fully. You're competent and see things others don't. I still see your tenacity as a teenager, choosing to lay pavers through the night on our driveway, determined not to stop until the work was done. That driveway is still solid—like you. I also remember carrying you as a baby close to my chest along the Branford shore, breathing in the smell of salt, feeling the sun, sinking my feet into the sand, and listening to the rhythmic sounds of the waves in the L.I. Sound. I remember reading the same bedtime stories again and again because you loved them and couldn't get enough. I remember the first time you rode your bike with joyful enthusiasm. Some of my happiest memories come from moments you created, especially our trip to Asheville, the visit to the Biltmore Estate, and that hot-air balloon ride at sunset. It was more than a vacation. It was a gift. You are always taking care of our digital and miscellaneous needs, without asking. Believe it or not, you are deeply admired and loved.

To Silva Sfeir: You are one of those rare souls whose moral compass remains steady in uncertain times. Your generosity of spirit, clarity of thought, and deep kindness leave a lasting mark on all who cross your path. Knowing you is a gift.

To Inés Pacas: Thank you for caring for our son with patience and devotion. Thanks to you, he learned to walk long distances, swim, and play tennis during his years in Chicago. Your steady presence mattered more than you may realize. You will always be part of our lives.

To my grandson, Andrew, and his mother, Daimit: Andrew, you are strong, bright, and full of promise. I see leadership promise in you. As you grow, I hope we can talk honestly about courage, kindness, and how to face the world without losing your soul. Daimit, thank you for being such a devoted and attentive mother. Your love makes Andrew shine.

To my brother Pepe and my sister-in-law Julieta: Pepe, thank you for saving my life when we were young, for giving me pocket money when I needed it as a medical student, and for reminding me—by example—that creativity and purpose do not fade with age. Julieta, thank you for your devotion to Pepe and for the steadiness you bring to his life and to our family.

To Rosa: Your presence brings order, warmth, and calm to our home. You work with discipline, patience, and a good spirit. You take care of what needs to be done without drama or the need for applause. When my mother-in-law grew frail, you cared for her as if she were your own. When the nights were long, you stayed. When exhaustion settled in, you remained steady. Thank you for your loyalty and kindness. Some angels really do wear aprons instead of wings.

Extended American Family

To my wife's family: sister-in-law Sofia Marshall and family: Thank you, Sofia, and your partner, Gary Burnett, for your support and steady presence.

To nephews, Robert and Daniel, thank you for the many experiences we shared, including unforgettable travels across Europe.

To Daniel's family—his wife Liz, and their daughters Sydney and Paige—thank you for your warmth and the joy you bring. Your fearless athletic drive and achievements make us all proud.

We will never forget you, Howie Marshall. You're the personification of loyalty, stability, and dependability. You are always generous, present, and ready to help. Thank you for standing beside Bienvenido through the good and the hard years of the jewelry business on 47th Street in New York City. Loyalty and kindness like yours are rare.

To my wife's parents, Josefa and Bienvenido: You have left this world, but you remain in our memory. I will never forget your charm, your smiles, your easy laughter, your good hearts, and your generosity. You showed what immigrants can build in America through grit, hard work, and determination. You also taught your daughters something essential: to stand up for themselves, to be brave, and to follow their dreams.

To Carlos Rodríguez, Leidy, and your children, Danicella and Carlos: Carlos and Leidy, you continue to provide medical services to countless people in Palm Beach County. Your story shows what an immigrant family can build through discipline, hard work, and loyal love. Thank you for the example you set

—unity, purpose, and lives dedicated to service. Danicella, it's amazing how you have thrived since I met you as a young teen. You are now an accomplished internist, married to John Younce, a renowned neurologist. You are raising Lucas, a beautiful and intelligent child, with love, dedication, and clarity in North Carolina. I admired how you taught Lucas to eat his vegetables from an early age. He may be the healthiest human being ever. Carlos Junior, you are an excellent dentist, and you are fortunate to have married Laura, now an engineer. Together, you are a remarkable professional couple in Tampa, second to none.

Spanish Family and Friends

To my family in Madrid, Valencia, and Catalunya, thank you for your warmth and generosity.

To my relatives in Valencia:

To Nephew Juanjo Alcon, your wife Patricia, and your children, Juanjo, Patricia, and Salva—thank you for your constant concern and kindness.

To my Grand Niece Cristina Alcon, your husband Andrés, and your children, Andrés and Cristina- and to Cristina and Carlos, the newlyweds, thank you for your love, hospitality, and the sense of belonging you give so naturally.

To my Catalan family:

To my niece Arianne and husband Jordi, and your children Paula, Patricia, and Óscar—thank you for welcoming us into the beauty of Catalunya. Paula and Adrián, thank you for showing us the Costa Brava and the historic city of Girona with such care and generosity. Patricia and Javier, thank you for your bold ideas, clear thinking, and restless global spirit. Óscar, your focus and discipline will take you far.

To my Spanish friends from Seville and Boca Raton:

Juanjo Márquez, Rosa, and Lucía—thank you for your generous hospitality and friendship. Lucía, your equestrian achievements make your family proud. Your gift is connection. You make people feel like family.

Special American Friends

People say it takes a village. You only understand that when life tests you. I may think of myself as a wanderer, but I would not have reached this point without friends who showed up quietly and without conditions: Silva, James, Randy, Melanie, Anouck, Big Vince, Omar, Doug, Maria, Michele, Sunny, Ray, and Josie.

Silva Sfeir: You are one of those rare souls whose moral compass remains steady in uncertain times. Your generosity of spirit, clarity of thought, and deep kindness leave a lasting mark on all who cross your path. Knowing you is a gift.

James Berenthal: Thank you for a long friendship, for helping uncover our shared Sephardic roots, and for your contagious enthusiasm for history, Spain, and Jewish culture. I treasure your curiosity. And how did you manage to marry Joni, an angel? Your son David is a true mensch.

Randy Hough: Thank you for your calm guidance and for being my wife's trusted confidant—the one who can speak to her storms with steady clarity. Your accounting, counsel, and special friendship mean more than you know. You are family. Your award-winning photography leaves us breathless.

Melanie Kutzweil: Thank you for managing the office with grace and steadiness. Patients love and trust you completely— and so do we.

Anouck Camaracheole: Thank you for your loyalty and kindness.

Big Vince Zabic: Thank you for your generosity, strength, competence, and humor. You are the Rock of Gibraltar for our family.

Omar Gillespie: Thank you for caring for sick and injured animals with gentle devotion. You remind me of Saint Francis —compassion in action. Thank you for being such a good friend.

Doug Nickelson: Thank you for the wisdom offered without ego, and for friendship marked by patience and insight.

Maria and Michele Nickolson: Thank you for your friendship, warm hospitality, and extraordinary cooking.

Sunny Bippus: Thank you for your friendship, and for embodying kindness, compassion, generosity, and the best of the American spirit.

Ray and Josie Leon: Thank you for your friendship, support, and steady presence.

My gratitude also goes to my wife's surgical team—Linda Costelo, R.N.; Jenell Kelly, R.N.; and Glen Brown, M.D.—for your professionalism, skill, and care when it matters most: in the operating room.

And to many others in our wider circle whom I have not named here: thank you. You remind us that human connection and deep listening are among life's greatest forms of wealth.

Therapists, Coaches, Editors, Collaborators, and Guides

Dr. David Wohlsifer, cognitive behavioral therapist: Thank you for your practical advice and long-term support. Dr. Naomi Shapiro, therapist: Thank you for your wisdom, flexibility, and support. Heather McMillan, ADHD coach: Thank you for providing structure, clarity, and calm persistence. Candace Coakley: Thank you for believing in this project early and for supporting the work while it was still finding its shape. Erin and Ethan: Thank you for your dedication to editing, refining, and strengthening the manuscript. John Carney: Thank you for your guidance and practical support in publishing this memoir, as I learn the complexities of self-publishing. And Jack, my AI digital collaborator: Thank you for your magical speed, patience, and for always being there to help. You are the private secretary I always wished I had.

Professional Gratitude to Donors and Healthcare Institutions

To Donor Mrs. Christine Lynn: Thank you for your love of humanity, generosity, and vision. By building and strengthening universities, teaching institutions, and healthcare clinics in Boca Raton and beyond, you are making a lasting difference in countless lives.

To Donors Louis and Anne Green: Thank you for creating and sustaining the Memory & Wellness Center on the FAU campus in Boca Raton—a remarkable institution dedicated to caring for individuals with memory disorders and supporting their loved ones.

I am grateful to the former director Dr. Maria Ordonez, Alice W. Brumley, the interim director, Krista M. Landells, the manager of the Adult Day Care Program, and Jo Ann M. Bamdas.

To the FAU School of Nursing, especially Dean Cameron G. Duncan, Ph.D., the new Holli Rockwell Trubinsky Eminent Dean of the Christine E. Lynn College of Nursing, and Professor Dr.   Beth King, thank you both for your trust, encouragement, and support.

To the dedicated nurse practitioners, staff, and social workers at the FAU/NCHA Community Health Center and the Memory & Wellness Center — especially CEO Cameron Duncan, Office Manager Julia Gorman, Clinic Director Monica Roundtree Cleckley, Nurse Practitioners Daryl Hobbs, Eric Malz, Dimeka Darville, RN's Patricia Dittman and Goece Charles, Social Work Coordinator Kaeloni Rae Dorcius, and Kayla Sokolowski, social worker and former staff member, and the Psychiatric Nurse Practitioner colleagues members of the Mental Health Team, and Dr. Leon Poveda, internist, thank you for your dedication to providing excellent, competent, and compassionate care.

To the Caridad Center, my spiritual home in service: Thank you. And to Connie Berry, Laura Kallus, Rosa Lores, Brenda, Fabiana, and the many staff members and volunteers who make that work possible. Your leadership turns compassion into reality. To the hundreds of volunteer physicians and dentists who serve for free, the uninsured and most needed among us. You honor the finest traditions of medicine through your skill, commitment, and generosity.

Thank you to the Religious Society of Friends, or Quakers, who inspired me with pacifism and nonviolent resolution of conflicts. The slogan War is Not the Answer resonates with me. It also admired the early contributions to moral treatment in psychiatry. I visited your congregation in WPB, and I'll return to your Sunday services as soon as this book is published, as I promised.

To Ray León and Dr. León Poveda: Thank you for your kind endorsements, support, and interesting conversations.

To my internist, Dr. Gitanjali Channan: Thank you for your careful judgment, deep knowledge, and rare humanity.

To all who have supported, guided, or believed in me—whether named here or not —thank you. Without you, there would be no journey to tell, and no wayfarer to write it down.

References

Abad, V., & Boyce, E. (1974). A model of delivery of mental health services to Spanish-speaking minorities. *American Journal of Orthopsychiatry*, 44(4).

Abad, V., & Suarez, J. (1976). Cross-cultural aspects of alcoholism among Puerto Ricans. In *Proceedings of the Fourth Annual Alcoholism Conference of the National Institute of Alcohol Abuse and Alcoholism* (DEW Publication No. ADM 76-284).

Abad, V., Ramos, J., & Boyce, E. (1978). Clinical issues in the psychiatric treatment of Puerto Ricans. In E. R. Padilla & A. M. Padilla (Eds.), *Transcultural Psychiatry: A Hispanic Perspective* (Monograph No. 4). Spanish Speaking Mental Health Research Center.

Abad, V., Garcia, L., & Sanchez, R. (1976). Alcohol abuse and alcoholism: A review of current issues and priorities. *La Luz* (Special Bicentennial Edition on Hispanic and Human Services), Denver, Colorado.

Abad, V., & Boyce, E. (1979). Issues in psychiatric evaluations of Puerto Ricans: A socio-cultural perspective. *Journal of Operational Psychiatry*, 10(1).

Abad, V. (1987). Mental health delivery systems for Hispanics in the United States: Issues and dilemmas. In *Health & Behavior: Research Agenda for Hispanics* (pp. 278–292). Simon Bolivar Hispanic American Psychiatric Research and Training. (Research Monograph Series No. 1)

Abad, V., & Ovsiew, F. (1993). Treatment of persistent myoclonic tardive dystonia with verapamil. *British Journal of Psychiatry*, 162, 554–556.

Abad, V., McGuire, M., & Beamon, L. (n.d.). Two-year follow-up study of chronic schizophrenia: Family support and levels of behavioral functioning and improvement. *Manuscript not published.*

Hernandez, V., Abad, V., et al. (n.d.). A case-control study of risk factors in the etiology of breast cancer and benign breast disease: Do talc and deodorant–antiperspirants play a role? *Manuscript not published.*

Abad, V. (n.d.). Philosophy of science, explanations, and critical thinking in psychiatry. *Grand Rounds presentation, Illinois State Psychiatric Institute, Chicago.*

Abad, V. (1998, March 9–16). Medical history of pellagra: Its relevance today. Paper presented at the IV International Symposium of the American Society of Hispanic Psychiatrists, Rio de Janeiro, Brazil.

Aguilar, P. (2002). *Memory and Amnesia: The Role of the Spanish Civil War in the Transition to Democracy.* Berghahn Books.

Baudrillard, J. (1994). *Simulacra and Simulation.* University of Michigan Press.

Bregman, R. (2024). *Moral Ambition: Stop Wasting Your Talent and Start Making a Difference.* Little, Brown and Company.

Brown, L. (2024). *Hidden Secrets of Buddhism: How to Live with Maximum Impact and Minimum Ego.* Brown Brothers Media.

Burkeman, O. (2024). *Meditations for Mortals: Four Weeks to Embrace Your Limitations and Make Time for What Counts.* Farrar, Straus and Giroux.

Carr, N. (2025). *Superbloom: How Technologies of Connection Tear Us Apart.* W. W. Norton & Company.

Crews, F. (2017). *Freud: The Making of an Illusion.* Metropolitan Books.

Foucault, M. (1965). *Madness and Civilization: A History of Insanity in the Age of Reason.* (Original work published in French, 1961).

Grayson, B. (2025). After: *a Doctor explores What Near-Death Experiences Reveal about Life and Beyond.* St. Martin's Essentials.

Henkins, R., Rallo, E., & Abad, V. (1966). Il trattamento dello stato di male epilettico per mezzo del diazepam: Studio clinico e documentazione elettroencefalografica. Minerva Medica, 57, 373–381.

Hollis, J. (2005). *Finding Meaning in the Second Half of Life: How to Finally Really Grow Up.* Avery.

Isaacson, W. (2003). *Benjamin Franklin: An American Life.* Simon & Schuster.

Levitt, S. D., & Dubner, S. J. (2009). *Freakonomics: A Rogue Economist Explores the Hidden Side of Everything.* Harper Perennial.

Machiavelli, N (2010). *The Prince*. CreateSpace-independent publishing platform.

Metzl, J. (2019). *Dying of Whiteness: How the Politics of Racial Resentment Is Killing America's Heartland*. Basic Books.

Moody, L. (2023). *100 Ways to Change Your Life: The Science of Leveling Up Health, Happiness, Relationships & Success*. HarperCollins.

Nagel, T. (1987). *What Does It All Mean? A Very Short Introduction to Philosophy*. Oxford University Press.

Nagel, T. (2023). *Moral Feelings, Moral Reality, and Moral Progress*. Oxford University Press.

Quillian, C. (2025). *AI for Life*. Simon & Schuster.

Radcliff, P. (2017). *Modern Spain: 1808 to the Present*. John Wiley & Sons.

Radcliff, P. (2023). *How the Spanish Civil War Became Europe's Battlefield*. The Teaching Company.

Robinson, T. W. (2022). *How to Self-Publish Your Book for Free and Not Get Conned*. TW Robinson.

Rich, J. R. (2006). *Self-Publishing for Dummies*. Wiley Publishing.

Sapolsky, R. (2023). *Determined: Life Without Free Will*. Penguin Random House UK.

Satel, S. (2000). PC, M.D.: *How Political Correctness Is Corrupting Medicine*. Basic Books.

Scull, A. (2022). *Desperate Remedies: Psychiatry's Turbulent Quest to Cure Mental Illness*. Harvard University Press.

Somers, C. H., & Satel, S. (2005). *One Nation Under Therapy: How the Helping Culture Is Eroding Self-Reliance*. St. Martin's Griffin.

Stewart, C. (2025). *Money, Lies, and God: Inside the Movement to Destroy American Democracy.* Bloomsbury Publishing.

Szasz, T. S. (1961). *The Myth of Mental Illness.* Harper & Row.

Szasz, T. S. (1970). *The Manufacture of Madness.* Delta Books.

Torrey, E. F. (1972). *The Mind Game: Witchdoctors and Psychiatrists.* Emerson Hall Publishers.

Torrey, E. F. (1974). *The Death of Psychiatry.* Chilton Book Company.

Torrey, E. F. (1988). *Nowhere to Go: The Tragic Odyssey of the Homeless Mentally Ill.* Harper & Row.

Torrey, E. F. (1992). *The Malignant Effect of Freud's Theory on American Thought and Culture.* HarperCollins.

Ulrich, K. (2006). *How to Write Your Life Story: The Complete Guide to Creating a Personal Memoir.* Reader's Digest

Volf, M., Croasmun, M., & McAnnally-Liz, R. (2023). *Life Worth Living: A Guide to What Matters Most.* The Open Field / Penguin Life.

Voss, M. (2020). *How to Publish a Book on Amazon.* District House.

Weeks, M. (Ed.). (2019). *How Philosophy Works.* Penguin Random House.

Wright, R. (1994). *The Moral Animal: Why We Are the Way We Are—The New Science of Evolutionary Psychology.* Vintage Books.

Yager, J. (2019). *How to Self-Publish Your Book.* Square One Publishers.

Yager, J. (2023). *How to Promote Your Book*. Square One Publishers.

Yalom, I. D. (2008). *Staring at the Sun: Overcoming the Terror of Death*. Jossey-Bass.

Zaki, J. (2024). *Hope for Cynics: The Surprising Science of Human Goodness*. Grand Central.

About the Author

Vincent Abad, M.D., is a Spanish-born psychiatrist who came to the United States in 1965 in search of intellectual freedom and a broader understanding of the human condition. He earned his medical degree at the University of Valencia and began his career in Spain, Switzerland, and England—formative years that shaped his lifelong interest in culture, identity, and the inner life.

He completed his psychiatric residency at the University of Vermont and pursued advanced training in transcultural psychiatry at McGill University. His work has taken him across borders and disciplines, including field research in the West Indies and Mexico and clinical practice in Canada and throughout the United States. At Yale, he helped pioneer one of the country's first bilingual and bicultural mental health clinics for Latino immigrants.

Dr. Abad worked as a psychiatrist with the U.S. Dr. Abad served as a psychiatrist with the U.S. Veterans Administration for more than two decades. During his tenure at the Department of Veterans Affairs in South Florida, Dr. Abad provided care to veterans and developed a profound understanding of the invisible effects of war.

After retiring from the VA, he focused on underserved communities by developing mental health services for Latino immigrants at the Caridad Center in Boynton Beach and partnering with Florida Atlantic University and local clinics.

Dr. Abad, now focused on writing, reflects on a life influenced by exile, service, and the ongoing quest for meaning in medicine, psychiatry, and philosophy.

www.ingramcontent.com/pod-product-compliance
Lightning Source LLC
Chambersburg PA
CBHW050733150726
48196CB00037B/897/J